HADRIAN'S WALL

History & Guide

Guy de la Bédoyère

TEMPUS

First published 1998, Reprinted 2000, 2001, 2005

Tempus Publishing Ltd
The Mill, Brimscombe Port
Stroud, Gloucestershire GL5 2QG
www.tempus-publishing.com

British Library Cataloguing in Publication Data.
A catalogue record for this book is available from the British Library.

ISBN 0 7524 1407 0

Typesetting and origination by Tempus Publishing.
Printed and bound in Great Britain.

Contents

Maps

N.B. Maps are sketch-maps and are not to scale. They are designed for guidance only.

Figures

Cover illustrations
Front: Cawfields milecastle, 42
Back: Silver *denarius* of Hadrian
Both copyright Guy de la Bédoyère

5

Foreword

This book developed out of several summers spent on the Hadrian's Wall system, exploring its numerous and fascinating features. There seemed to be a need for a book which covered both the history and the archaeology as well as serving as a practical guide to seeing what remains. The Wall can now be seen at its best since antiquity thanks to the efforts of antiquarians, the imaginative and stimulating work by modern archaeologists, and the guardianship of English Heritage and local authorities. During the preparation of this book in 1997 I was also involved in recording the Radio 4 series *The Romans in Britain* and had the good fortune to talk to noted Wall scholars Lindsay Allason-Jones and Dr Jim Crow of the University of Newcastle, Dr Paul Bidwell at South Shields, Dr Brian Dobson of the University of Durham, and Robin Birley, Director at Vindolanda. Much of the book has benefited from the conversations we had. I would like to thank particularly Peter Kemmis Betty for inviting me to write this book, and both him and Pat Southern, a highly-experienced guide to the Wall and Roman scholar, for so carefully reading the finished manuscript and pointing out errors and making many immensely valuable suggestions.

Although every effort has been made to ensure the accuracy of the information in this book it will be obvious that even in a short time orientation of roads, times of admission or telephone numbers may change. Moreover, and more importantly, no one visiting the Wall should assume that access is automatically possible unless explicitly stated so at the locations. Fortunately, this is normally obvious thanks to clear English Heritage or footpath signs.

Hadrian's Wall is amongst the most exciting monuments of the whole ancient world, west and east, to survive. It has given me enormous pleasure since my first visit in the late 1960s. I hope this book helps others to enjoy it as much.

Guy de la Bédoyère
Eltham, November 1997

How to use this book

This book is designed for visitors who have access to transport of any sort, and intend to visit Hadrian's Wall on a single day, or several different days. Lying mostly between Newcastle and Carlisle, the Wall is relatively easily visited by car, motorcycle, bicycle, and public transport. Both Newcastle and Carlisle are on main-line railway routes from the south and north, and are connected by a cross-country route with stations at Hexham, Haydon Bridge, Bardon Mill, Haltwhistle, and Brampton. In the summer months local buses run from Hexham, Haltwhistle, and Carlisle stations to the Wall.

The division into chapters draws together parts of the Wall which can be easily seen in a short day, two chapters in a single long day. Much will depend on the time of year and the weather. In summer long days on the Wall can be particularly rewarding but even in sunny conditions the strength of the wind can be rather debilitating after several hours. The book is designed to be equally useful for visitors walking the Wall from one end to the other. The text is intended to be practical and straightforward while 'on location', but reading in advance should prove profitable. Sections of the Wall which are no longer visible or accessible are generally outside the scope of this book unless they are of special interest and relevant to understanding the Wall system.

For readers who wish to understand the archaeology and history of the Wall in greater depth an appendix of Sources is provided; this details the principal literary references to the Wall and the more important Roman monumental inscriptions. A Glossary also covers some of the more commonly-used technical and Roman terms which crop up.

Sites

Major Wall sites are indicated in **bold** type, for example HOUSESTEADS (principal forts, and museums) and **Banks East Turret** (Wall features such as milecastles and turrets). These are either museums, or locations where remains are properly signposted from the main road and usually have designated parking facilities. Full details of access are provided under the heading. Other features are indicated by capitals, for example LIMESTONE CORNER. These are places, often of some interest, but which are not instantly or easily accessible.

Finds from the various sites have generally been removed to one of three museums: The Museum of Antiquities in Newcastle upon Tyne, Chesters Museum, and Tullie House Museum in Carlisle. In the text these are referred to as Newcastle, Chesters, and Carlisle respectively. Brief descriptions are given where appropriate in the route along the Wall. Most other finds are deposited at Housesteads site museum, Vindolanda site museum, Carvoran Roman Army Museum, South Shields Arbeia Roman Fort Museum, and in London at the British Museum.

Although the Wall can largely be walked for free, the forts and museums mostly carry admission charges. One cost-effective method of covering the cost is to join English Heritage as a member (contact their Customer Services Department at PO Box 9019, London W1A 0JA. Tel: 0171–973–3434). This is good value for families and will take care of Chesters, Housesteads, and Birdoswald. However, this solution does not cover Vindolanda (though English Heritage members receive a modest discount), Carvoran Roman Army Museum, and Tullie House in Carlisle. Wallsend, Newcastle, and South Shields are free. Not everywhere is open all year but the major sites at Housesteads, Corbridge, and Chesters are.

Local tourist information is available on 01434 605555 or 01228 606003 (Hexham), and 01228 512444 (Carlisle). Information on the Hadrian's Wall bus (all year round, but reduced service in winter) is available from 01434 605555 or 01228 606003.

Maps

Ordnance Survey maps are best for exploring the Wall. Throughout the text full grid references are given. A small number of simple sketch maps (not to scale) are included in this book, designed only for guidance. The 1989 edition of the Ordnance Survey's *Historical Map and Guide* to *Hadrian's Wall* is quite handy for general information but difficult to use. The 1972 version is easier to read and much more useful. More practical on the whole are the standard 1:50 000 Series maps. Numbers 85–88 cover the Wall area with 86 and 87 relevant to the central sector (including a large overlap) where most of the important Wall sites are. The Pathfinder 1:25 000 Series maps are the best but their cost and limited area coverage make them an expensive option. Pathfinder 546 'Haltwhistle & Gilsland', however, covers all the way from Housesteads to Birdoswald. For the Newcastle area the Geographers' A–Z Map Company's *AZ street atlas* for the area is indispensable and includes a map of the Metro network on the back cover.

Equipment and clothing

Land management along the Wall means that designated sites are equipped with maintained footpaths and stiles over field walls and fences. However, the Wall crosses spectacular stretches of up-country and there are some places, especially in the central sector, where small children and those unsure on their feet may have difficulty. Wet-weather clothing is essential, as is a good pair of walking shoes, and it is usually a good idea to carry drinking water and some food.

1. Introduction:
the history of the Wall

Any nation's power is limited by the capacity of its government to control land and its inhabitants. In early modern times the expansion of seapower made it feasible for certain small and geographically insignificant countries to control phenomenal quantities of territory. In the ancient world it was virtually impossible for any ruler to exercise more than the most superficial control over his or her possessions. Empires rose and fell on the caprices of personality and circumstance. The Roman Empire was different because its organization and military power gave it the potential to exist beyond the personality of the emperor. Despite limited technology and communications, Rome had conquered and could manage the government of the largest empire that Europe or western Asia had yet seen. However, Hadrian (**1**) recognized that the Empire could not expand indefinitely and decided to consolidate its frontiers. His Wall in northern Britain is one of the most important monuments to that change of policy.

The meandering line of the Wall and its associated structures represent a considerable achievement for a non-industrial society. The supremely energetic Victorians thought it something only comparable with their railway projects. In an age conscious of cost and profit we see it as a prohibitively expensive prospect. In the middle ages it was regarded with a different kind of incredulity. To the monks and wanderers in the north the Romans had been metaphorical (if not literal) giants, capable of anything and everything.

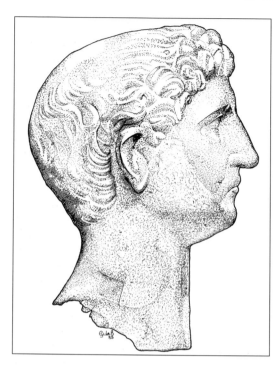

1   Bronze bust of Hadrian (117–38) from the Thames in London. Probably from a monumental statue set up to commemorate the emperor's visit in or around 122. Height 410mm.

EARLY DESCRIPTIONS

Occasional references in early post-Roman texts show that the Wall was familiar to travellers, though remoteness made it a wild and frightening place to visit. Bede, writing at Jarrow in the early 700s, thought, like the earlier chronicler Gildas, that it had been built to defend Britain in the last days of Roman rule, replacing what was believed to be an earlier turf wall by Septimius Severus (193–211). Bede had certainly seen the Wall and described it as 12ft (3.65m) high and 8ft (2.43m) thick (Source 23).

The first major account of the Wall was by William Camden (1551–1623) in his book *Britannia*. In 1599 he visited the Wall for himself, publishing his observations in the edition of 1600. He announced that: 'I my selfe have beheld with my owne eyes ... huge peeces thereof standing for a great way together, only wanting their battlements'. He thought that the rearward ditch and mound system of the Wall, now called the Vallum, had been built by Hadrian as an earth rampart frontier (this was the component attributed by Bede to Severus). Camden had the benefit of published ancient texts and realized Hadrian had been involved, but still attributed the stone Wall, a short (but variable) distance to the north, to Severus. This book remained available in various, posthumously-revised, editions throughout the eighteenth century. Further accounts were issued by Alexander Gordon in his *Itinerarium Septentrionale* (1726), John Horsley (1685–1732) in his *Britannia Romana* (1732), William Stukeley (1687–1765) in his *Iter Boreale* published posthumously in

1776 and based on notes made in 1725. What was perhaps the first guidebook to the Wall, the *Vallum Romanum* of John Warburton (1682–1759), appeared in 1753; its author described it as a 'pocket companion' for 'learned travellers' to the 'famous Picts Wall'.

In 1745 the forces of Charles Stuart, 'the Young Pretender', in the Jacobite Rebellion entered England in the last serious attempt to restore the Catholic descendant of James II to the throne of England. They marched south down the west coast and took Carlisle. Troops stationed at Newcastle under the command of Field-Marshal George Wade (1673–1748) were unable to engage them in time, because there was no adequate cross-country road. Wade lost his command as a result but he had already made his name as a military road-builder in Scotland. The Wall was identified as an excellent solution: its demolition provided hard-core and the foundations served as a solid base for the new Military Road. It was not begun until 1752, four years after Wade's death, but it had presumably been his idea. A long section of Wall west from Newcastle suffered accordingly to the horror of William Stukeley who described the demolition in his *Medallic History of Carausius*, published in the late 1750s.

In 1801 William Hutton (1723–1815), a topographer and bookseller from the Midlands, visited the Wall. His account, published in various editions in the early 1800s, provides a graphic record of the Wall's demolition in order to build farmhouses. John Hodgson (1779–1845), vicar of Jarrow, looked at inscriptions that had been found by chance along the Wall and realized that Hadrian and not Severus must have been responsible for the curtain's original construction in stone. Hodgson published the idea in the *History of Northumberland* (1840). This coincided with an increased awareness of classicism in north-western Europe generally; thereafter the Wall was examined more systematically. The lives of two antiquaries, John Clayton (1792–1890) and John Collingwood Bruce (1805–92), represented a turning point in the fortunes of the Wall. Excavations and clearances took place at various sites. Gradually the details of the Wall system with its forward ditch, rearward Vallum, forts, milecastles, and turrets, began to emerge.

Collingwood Bruce enshrined the progress on the Wall in his survey called *The Roman Wall*, first published in 1851. Subsequently he produced the *Handbook to the Roman Wall* (1863), various revised editions of which have appeared over the years. It opened up the idea that the Wall and all its associated features should be studied as a whole. Generations of scholars subsequently built their careers on the Wall, and this continues to the present time. There has been so much work on the Wall since the middle of the nineteenth century that it is impossible adequately to summarise here what has been written. But the following description of the Wall should help to give an idea of how Hadrian's Wall is understood at the moment as a result of their, and more recent, work.

THE HISTORICAL BACKGROUND BEFORE THE WALL

At no time during the Roman occupation of Britain did military control extend over the whole island. Claudius invaded in AD 43 and during the rest of his reign and that of his successor Nero (54–68) the army established control of the south and east. But the northern part proved more difficult to suppress. The terrain was harder, the winters fiercer, and the supply routes longer. During the reigns of Vespasian, Titus, and Domitian (69–96) considerable advances were made into northern Britain, principally during the governorship of Agricola (c.77–83/4) who reached almost as far as the Moray Firth but these conquests were never consolidated. As a result the frontier of Britannia always lay within the island.

After Agricola's most northerly conquests were abandoned by Domitian in c.86/7 Roman policy in Britain becomes difficult to understand because there are practically no historical references or stone inscriptions from the whole of Trajan's reign (98–117). This highlights the inadequacy of archaeology under such circumstances and, realistically, we have to accept that the beginning part of the second century is something of a 'dark age'. But it seems that between c.100–110 some of the remaining outpost forts in southern Scotland were destroyed either by attackers, or by Romans withdrawing. The background seems to have been British wars, and a reduction of the Roman army in Britain to strengthen garrisons elsewhere, in particular to contribute to Trajan's wars of conquest in south-eastern Europe and the East.

A number of military installations between, and including, Corbridge and Carlisle appear to belong roughly to the years 90–120. They may have formed a frontier zone based on the contemporary east-west road known now as the Stanegate, though whether they were conceived as a 'frontier' is quite another matter. If so, Hadrian's Wall may have been designed as a re-working of the idea, but based on an actual wall.

THE BUILDING OF HADRIAN'S WALL

The original design

Hadrian (117–38) appreciated that Roman military conquest could not continue indefinitely. The wars of Trajan in Dacia and Parthia had been militarily expensive and protracted. Hadrian abandoned some of Trajan's conquests and decided to stabilize the frontiers by exploiting natural features such as rivers, and filling in the gaps with fortifications made of earthen turf ramparts and timber palisades like those in Germany. Hadrian's Wall belongs to this general range of contemporary frontier works but formed a uniquely coherent group of military works. Also, its eastern half was built in stone and later the western turf stretch was replaced with a stone wall too.

At the beginning of Hadrian's reign Britain was still far from peaceful, and a later reference suggests that many soldiers were lost (Source 1a). Coins of c.119 depict Britannia in a 'defeated' pose (**2**), an image which is being

*2   Bronze coin (as) of Hadrian of
c. 119–22, depicting the female personification
of 'Britannia' in submissive or defeated pose.*

supported more and more by recent discoveries. In or about 122 Hadrian
visited Britain where his fourth-century biographer says '[Hadrian] reformed
many things, and, the first [to do so], erected a wall over a length of 80 miles,
which was to force apart the Romans and barbarians' (Source 1b). That,
unfortunately, is it as far as Roman historians go, though coins of the reign
depict Hadrian visiting Britain and speaking to the army there. The Latin word
used for 'was to force apart' is *divideret* and means something rather stronger
than just 'separate' or 'divide', which is how it is often translated. The word has
contributed to a belief that the Wall created a simple linear barrier between
civilization and barbarian chaos. In reality the situation was far more complex,
not least for the reason that the area behind the Wall was as troublesome and
insecure as the area beyond it. Strangely, the preceding passage in Hadrian's
biography is rarely commented on. It describes how the emperor arrived in
Britain from Germany where he had toughened up the garrison. He had
ordered the demolition of any fort facility which smacked of good living like
ornamental gardens, or even dining rooms. He also enforced a harder but fairer
regime of military discipline and administration, and ordered improvements in
equipment.

It is possible that Hadrian introduced the same reforms in Britain. The
biographer adds that Hadrian put right many problems in the province, but
does not specify them. The thirty years of intermittent withdrawal from

3   *Inscription from milecastle 38 (Hotbank) attributing the structure to the II Legion*
Augusta *during the reign of Hadrian and the governorship of Aulus Platorius Nepos (c. 122–6).*
See Source 2.

around the year 87 was long enough for many soldiers in Britain to have done little more than experience the demoralizing effects of sporadic defeats or of serving as vegetating garrisons for their entire careers. It's a mistake to believe that the Wall was necessarily a knee-jerk response to an immediate threat, in spite of the evidence for a war around the years 117–19 (Source 1a–c) . The real purpose of an army is to keep the peace, not sustain war, and the Wall grew out of a change in policy on how to achieve that.

The Wall, despite being devised as a strategic and political tool, would also have involved the troops in all the homogenising and morale-boosting competitive side-effects of mutual participation in a major project. Hadrian had a personal interest in architecture so the scheme might have been based at least in part on his ideas. Building began under the governor Aulus Platorius Nepos, a personal friend of Hadrian's. He may have accompanied Hadrian from Germany but was certainly in his post by the summer of 122 (Sources 2–4). In or around the year 126 or 127 he was succeeded by Trebius Germanus who might have continued the Wall's construction but remains to be testified on the Wall itself (Sources 6 and 25).

The frontier was conceived as a stone wall 10 Roman feet (about 3m) broad with a forward ditch separated by a berm about 20 Roman feet (5.9m) wide. It was to run from the river Tyne in what is now central Newcastle to the river Irthing at Willowford. This is now known as the 'Broad Wall'. Roughly every Roman mile there was a small stone fort, which we call a 'milecastle', attached to the south side of the Wall. Access to the milecastle was by a gate in its south wall, or from the north through a gate in the Wall itself. Between each pair of

4   *Centurial stone from Carrawburgh recording the construction of 24 paces (P XXIIII) of fort rampart by a century under the command of Thrupo.*

milecastles two small towers, or 'turrets', were placed at approximately $\frac{1}{3}$-mile intervals. From Willowford the Wall was continued westwards in turf to Bowness-on-Solway, and included turf milecastles and stone turrets. The total length was 80 Roman miles (74 statute miles or 118km) but the system of milecastles and turrets, probably connected by a wooden palisade, continued down the Cumbrian coast.

Inscriptions from the Wall show that it was mostly built by detachments of the II *Augusta*, VI *Victrix* (which appears to have been brought over by Hadrian himself), and XX *Valeria Victrix* Legions (**3**; Source 2). Each built stretches about 5–6 miles (8–10km) long, distinguished by differences in structural detail. Sharing the work amongst the legions was of course a practical use of manpower, but it was also bound to create a sense of productive rivalry and inject a dynamic of internal co-operation which might have galvanized the individual parties into more cohesive disciplined units (**4**).

The milecastles and turrets are now numbered from the east of the Wall at Wallsend, starting with milecastle 1, but those in the far eastern sector are largely theoretical or only known from antiquarian references. Turrets are numbered westwards from each milecastle, thus milecastle 37, turrets 37a, 37b, milecastle 38 and so on. Quite significant variations in distances between the milecastles and turrets were allowed. For example milecastles 38 and 39 are separated by 0.94 of a mile, and 39 and 40 by 1.11 miles. Milecastles which have been excavated rarely produce traces of accommodation for more than a dozen soldiers; even taking the turrets into account this allows for a very small Wall garrison of around 1000–1500 troops.

5   *The eastern wing-wall of milecastle 48 (Poltross Burn) looking west towards the mile-castle. The horizontal off-set where the Narrow Wall has been built on a Broad Wall foundation can be seen, as can the vertical off-set where the Broad wing-wall of the milecastle meets the Narrow Wall.*

If this was indeed how the Wall was designed to begin with, it was never completed in this form. Before construction had been underway for very long, major changes were made.

DEVELOPMENTS UNDER HADRIAN

Narrowing the Wall

By around 123–4 some stretches of Wall had only been built to a couple of courses in height, while other sections were still at foundation level or not even laid out. A decision was made to continue on a narrower gauge. The new design is known now as the 'Narrow Wall', and though nominally 8 Roman feet wide there is actually considerable variation, sometimes to less than 7ft (2.1m) wide (though some of this may be due to subsequent repair and rebuilding). Where foundations and the lower courses of the Wall, as well as some milecastles and turrets, or only parts of, had already been prepared for the Broad Wall the change in thickness is quite clear (**5**). Occasionally, for example near milecastle 39, the Narrow Wall was built on a different alignment, and required new foundations. Clearly the narrowing of the Wall will have saved time, manpower, and stone. Perhaps the workload had been underestimated, or

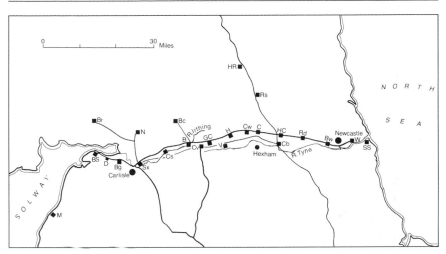

Map 1 *Map of northern Britain showing Hadrian's Wall, the principal forts and major modern towns. From east to west:* **SS** *South Shields,* **W** *Wallsend,* **Bw** *Benwell,* **Rd** *Rudchester,* **HC** *Haltonchesters,* **Cb** *Corbridge,* **C** *Chesters,* **Cw** *Carrawburgh,* **H** *Housesteads,* **V** *Vindolanda,* **GC** *Greatchesters,* **Cv** *Carvoran,* **B** *Birdoswald,* **Cs** *Castlesteads,* **Sx** *Stanwix,* **Bg** *Burgh by Sands,* **D** *Drumburgh,* **BS** *Bowness-on-Solway. To the north:* **Rs** *Risingham,* **HR** *High Rochester,* **Bc** *Bewcastle,* **N** *Netherby,* **Br** *Birrens. To the south-west:* **M** *Maryport.*

perhaps Nepos was anxious to have the project completed during his governorship and thus maximise his prestige. It may also have been connected with the building of the forts. Some sections, not yet laid-out, were built around now entirely on the Narrow gauge and this included an eastern extension from Newcastle to Wallsend.

The forts

More significant than narrowing the Wall was the building of forts along it. These were at (from east to west): Wallsend, Newcastle, Benwell, Rudchester, Haltonchesters, Chesters, Housesteads, Greatchesters, Birdoswald, Castlesteads (exceptionally, not attached to the Wall), Stanwix, Burgh by Sands, Drumburgh, and Bowness-on-Solway (Map 1; Sources 3–5). Carrawburgh fort, between Chesters and Housesteads, was added later but probably still under Hadrian. The process was advanced enough by 125–6 for building inscriptions bearing Aulus Platorius Nepos' name to be erected at some forts (Sources 3 and 4). That his successor Trebius Germanus (Source 6) is not yet testified on the Wall (or anywhere else) suggests that construction of the Wall and forts was fairly advanced by 126, notwithstanding the subsequent additions and alterations.

On rare occasions fort names appear on altars found on or near the sites. An altar to Silvanus from Birdoswald names the unit responsible as the *Venatores Banniess[es]*, the 'Hunters of Banna'. Other names come from medieval copies of older documents, such as the late-Roman military gazetteer, *Notitia Dignitatum*. It listed military commands across the Empire including those *per*

17

lineam valli ('along the course of the Wall'), and the units and their bases under those commands. These written records are compromised by omissions, mistakes, and a lack of evidence for the dates of the places and units being referred to. Some useful visual evidence comes from a pair of bronze utensils, apparently souvenirs of the Wall and known as the Rudge cup (see below; **7**) and the Amiens skillet. Both bear stylized depictions of the Wall and name forts in the western sector of the Wall starting *a Mais* 'from *Maiae*' (Bowness-on-Solway), *Aballava* (Burgh by Sands), *Uxelodunum* (Stanwix), *Camboglans* (Castlesteads), *Banna* (Birdoswald); the Amiens skillet adds *Esica* (*Aesica*; Greatchesters). They were probably sold alongside similar goods which completed the series of names.

In some places building the forts meant demolishing stretches of the newly-built Wall, and even turrets and milecastles. This seems wasteful and manifest proof that the Wall had been begun on the basis that the Stanegate forts would house the main garrisons. This is the so-called 'fort decision', an inferred drastic change of plan. It is certainly a reasonable inference. But, equally feasible explanations are that the order to begin construction of the Wall was taken in the knowledge that the fort sites were yet to be surveyed; or, the forts were planned from the beginning but had not originally been conceived as physically joined to the Wall.

Whatever the scheme had been, the new forts were sited on the Wall very roughly around 7–8 Roman miles (about 10–12km) apart. Each was normally built projecting in part to the north, or up against the Wall to the south, and was to be manned by an auxiliary unit (see The Army of the Wall below). The Stanegate was mostly too far to the south ever to have been a useful home for the main Wall garrison. But none of this provides us with a break-down of Wall policy and planning. All we can say is that construction of the forts did not begin until the building of the Wall had been underway for a while, and that the forts' construction *as executed* required demolition of existing features; whether that was a *change* of plan or simply a stage in a consecutive series of anticipated procedures designed to allow flexibility as the Wall progressed are conclusions that we lack the evidence to make.

The Vallum and additional forts

Around the time forts were introduced the Vallum was added. This flat-bottomed ditch, 20 Roman feet (5.9m) wide and 20 feet deep, was flanked by 10 feet (3m) high and 20 feet wide mounds 30 feet (8.9m) away on either side. It created a 120 foot (35m) wide system of earthworks. It ran south of the Wall and in post-Roman times was mistaken for a frontier in its own right, being called a *vallum* (which in fact means a 'rampart' or 'wall'). Although the forward ditch, north of the Wall, was sometimes omitted depending on local conditions, the Vallum was constructed regardless. In general it lay around 120 Roman feet (about 35m) behind the Wall but this varies considerably. The Vallum, together with the Wall, demarcated a 'military zone' or 'corridor'. Crossings were built opposite the forts (but not the milecastles) and this

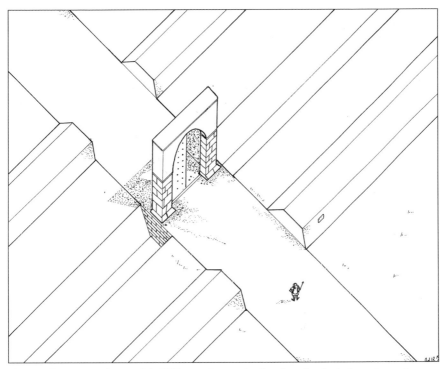

6   *Reconstructed view of the Vallum and a crossing based on the physical remains to the south of the fort at Benwell.*

suggests that the Vallum was also devised as a means of funnelling trans-Wall traffic into easily-policed channels (**6**).

The Vallum usually diverts round forts. It was thus dug either with full knowledge of where the forts were to be built and at the same time, or shortly afterwards. So, it skirts to the south of Benwell and even the detached fort at Castlesteads. The Vallum may have formed part of the original plan but was perhaps not scheduled to be constructed until the curtain was substantially complete. It lies backfilled underneath the fort of Carrawburgh which must therefore have been added later, but probably not much later, to fill the long gap between Chesters and Housesteads (Source 5). Oddly, no new stretch of Vallum diverting around Carrawburgh was dug. This suggests that by the time the fort was built it was no longer considered quite so vital; on the Antonine Wall system (see below) the Vallum was omitted. The Stanegate fort of Carvoran, further west between Greatchesters and Birdoswald, was now apparently rebuilt in stone to guard a river valley (Sources 7, 8); the Vallum diverts to its north, showing that the fort was not incorporated within the Wall system but also that, like Castlesteads, it was already in existence and had to be skirted.

Replacing the Turf Wall in stone

During Hadrian's reign the stretch of Turf Wall near Birdoswald was rebuilt in stone; the rest was probably replaced at the same time or later in the second century. The new milecastles tend to be larger than those built to the east and other improvements such as regular drains were introduced. At Birdoswald, which had projected north of the Turf Wall, the new stone Wall was built on a slightly different alignment to meet the fort's north wall, thus placing the whole fort to the south of the Wall (**59**). This has allowed examination of the Turf Wall nearby. It was made of cut turfs sometimes laid on a cobbled base 20 Roman feet (5.9m) wide, and sometimes directly onto the subsoil. Its original height and finish are unknown but like the stone Wall, in order to have been effective, it would have had to have been around at least 10–13ft (3–4m) high, and probably supported a timber palisade. A continuous stone base would have increased stability and improved drainage. There was nothing particularly unsatisfactory about using turf; the technique is fast and durable and it was the normal method of building Roman frontiers.

The details of all these various changes are unknown, including the length of time involved. The Wall was inevitably subject to continuous repair and all sorts of local problems attributable to weather, the units responsible, and unforeseen difficulties at specific locations. These would have resulted in a frontier which must have spent years looking like a building site, with some finished sections and other parts in a state of semi-dereliction. At Birdoswald recent analysis of environmental evidence suggests that the fort was begun and then abandoned long enough for scrub to grow over the site. When construction resumed here the scrub had to be burnt off.

The Wall is unlikely to have been welcomed by local inhabitants who must have spent some of their time harrying the builders, perhaps by stealing materials, or burning timber stocks. There is no evidence for this but the capacity of technologically-inferior communities to irritate their conquerors is well known in other places and at other times.

THE WALL STRUCTURES

The curtain

From Wallsend in the east as far as the Irthing the Wall was built of local limestone. When the stretch of Turf Wall to the west of the Irthing was replaced in stone, limestone was used for the first 7 miles (11km), and then the softer local red sandstone for the remainder. All the stone came from numerous quarries near the Wall and traces of many can still be seen.

Building started with a stone foundation on which two or three courses of facing blocks were set in place on either side with a lime-based mortar. The gap was then filled with rubble and 'puddled clay', a clay or clay and sand preparation mixed with water and lime which dries to a watertight state. Then another two or three layers of facing stones were laid, the gap filled as before

7 *The Rudge cup (width 50mm) which appears to depict a stylized representation of the Wall. The 'towers' have crenellations and thus may be the north gates of forts, the north towers of milecastles, or even turrets. The symbols between may show shield decoration. A band at the top names forts in the western sector:* Camboglans *is* Castlesteads.

and so on. The first-century BC Roman architect Vitruvius describes this kind of construction as prone to a shorter life than one built of dressed stone throughout, and only used by men in a hurry (*On Architecture* II.viii.7, 8); this certainly helps explain the comprehensive rebuilding of the curtain in some areas in the early third century. To relieve pressure from water ponding in natural dips drains were built into the structure. Similar arrangements allowed streams to run under the Wall. Exposure of some long-buried sections has shown that whitewash and/or a hard white lime mortar may have been used to cover the whole curtain, perhaps to make the frontier conspicuous from a distance, to resist weathering, and to make sections which needed repair more visible.

None of the Wall stands to its original height today, and nor has it done in recorded post-Roman times. Unfortunately, Bede and other early antiquarian commentators provide a variety of different figures for the height ranging from 12 to 21ft (3.7–6.4m) (Source 23), as a result of guesswork, casual measurements, and different degrees of survival. But the original planned height can be estimated. At Willowford the Hadrianic bridge over the Irthing was prepared on Broad Wall measurements. The wing wall here was built in descending step form to make an easy join when the Wall was built up to it. Restoring the angle of the wing-wall step (which can be distinguished because the Wall was finished in Narrow form here) back up to the bridge suggests a height of around 11–13ft (3.5–4m) for the Broad Wall. Having said that it is, of course, quite possible that the Wall was not of consistent height throughout its

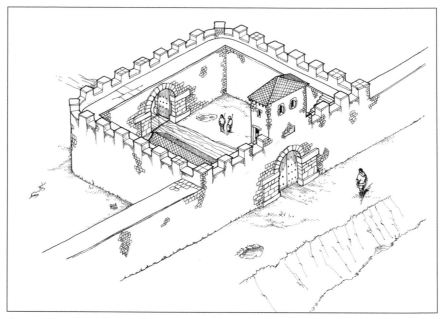

8   *Reconstructed view of a 'short axis' milecastle, based on the physical remains of milecastle 37 (Housesteads west). The form of the gate tower is completely speculative. Unlike normal reconstructions the Wall is shown here with patchy white rendering (which is testifed), and without crenellations (which are not).*

length, either as a matter of design or as a result of not being completed; the Narrow Wall, for instance, may very well have been lower than the Broad Wall. Some further evidence survives at the milecastles (see below). At Thorny Doors, east of Cawfields (**48**), the Wall stands to about 10ft (3.1m), one of the highest surviving points.

Whether the Wall had a walkway and a parapet or not has always been a matter for debate. Nobody knows. None of the antiquarian sources ever describes a part of the Wall with a parapet. No collapsed section of parapet has ever been found. Scattered capstones for crenellations occasionally turn up, but usually near milecastles or turrets, which rather suggests that if they had parapets the Wall did not but this is hardly proof either way.

The Rudge cup (**7**) and the Amiens skillet bear the only images of the Wall from antiquity. The cup depicts vertical structures with crenellations. The wall shown in between has no crenellations. It is thus probably showing the turrets, milecastle north gates, or the north gates of forts named on the cup. In any case there is no evidence that the maker of the cup or skillet had ever been to the Wall; while they may well be souvenirs manufactured and sold along the frontier, nothing like them has ever been found on or near the Wall. Building and maintaining a walkway with a parapet would certainly have added to the scale of work which the Wall demanded. If these are all good reasons for saying that the Wall probably had no walkway and parapet there are many equally

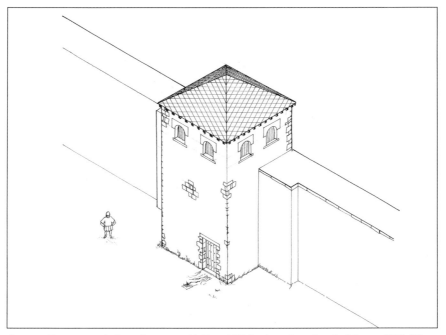

9   *Reconstructed view of a turret with Broad Wall wings abutted to the Narrow Wall. The wing walls are shown full height but need not have been. The form of the turret's roof is speculative. Some reconstructions show turrets with external wooden galleries. As with **8** Wall crenellations are omitted.*

good arguments for the contrary; the bridges at Chesters and Willowford, for instance, were wide enough to carry roads and were physical continuations of the Wall. Perhaps the Wall was planned with a walkway and parapet but this was either never executed, or was only added at certain points. We will probably never know.

The milecastles and turrets

Milecastles were miniature forts attached to the south face of the Wall and were equipped with sheltered accommodation (**8**). Each enclosed an area of only around 250–300 square metres and was little more than a fortified double gateway through the Wall. Inscriptions, styles of gate, and ground-plans have made it possible to distinguish the work of the legions. The II *Augusta*, for example, is associated with massive masonry gates and ground-plans where the east-west axis is greater than the north-south axis (Source 2). The north gates, and perhaps the south, may have had towers, though their form is difficult to reconstruct. Evidence for milecastle barracks varies. A minimum of 12 soldiers has been suggested but in one or two cases more than 30 could have been accommodated. The surviving part of a flight of steps at Poltross Burn (milecastle 48) suggests, if extended at the same angle, that its rampart walkway was 15ft (4.6m) from the ground (**56**). The remains of the north gate at milecastle 37 are consistent with this (**46**). But they only provide evidence for milecastles, not necessarily the Wall.

Turrets were even simpler and were not equipped with gates through the Wall. They probably had at least two floors, the upper of which was reached either by ladder or wooden stairs (**9**). They may also have had external platforms on the upper level. Normally the turrets were recessed into the Wall; pre-Wall look-out towers like Pike Hill (west of Birdoswald fort) were incorporated into the Wall which was diverted to meet them while later additions, like that at Peel Gap (between the forts at Housesteads and Greatchesters), were just tacked on to the curtain.

There is no conclusive evidence for the roofing of either milecastle gates or turrets. Fragments of window-glass reported from some milecastles and turrets indicate that they were roofed somehow. Roof slates with nail holes have been found at turrets 29b and 44b, but the Peel Gap tower has produced a capstone indicating it had crenellations. The Rudge cup suggests they had crenellations. It is not entirely easy to accept the idea of flat roofs in Britain. Apart from personal comfort there is the problem of structural maintenance of flat-roofed buildings, particularly in such exposed places. The general evidence from Trajan's Column (see Glossary) is that timber superstructures of gates might be flat-roofed but many of the stone structures and free-standing towers portrayed had pitched roofs. Perhaps both flat and pitched roofs were employed on the Wall, simultaneously and at different times.

The forts

The forts either straddle the Wall or sit immediately behind it with their north ramparts forming a continuation of the Wall. The single exception is Castlesteads which lies between Wall and Vallum. They vary in size from 2 acres (0.8ha) at Drumburgh to 9.3 acres (3.7ha) at Stanwix. The average is around 5 acres (2ha). A projecting fort had three twin-portalled gates to the north of the Wall, and one to the south, supplemented by a pair of single-portalled gates. A fort to the rear of the Wall had four twin-portalled gates. Depending on the state of the Wall in the location where it was built a fort's ramparts either were, or were not, bonded with the curtain. Each usually contained a headquarters building in the centre and an adjacent house for the commanding officer. Around them were granaries, stables (if required), barracks, and other facilities like a hospital, ovens, and latrines. Forts are archaeologically far more complex than the milecastles and turrets because the buildings were subject to much more substantial phases of rebuilding. However, they tend to be fairly typical in form making it possible for selective archaeology to produce a fairly complete form, for example at Wallsend (**15**).

Was the Wall finished?

The Wall may never really have been completed. Various distractions, such as sickness or the need for troops elsewhere at any given time, could quite easily have seriously compromised building. The logistics must have been remarkable and an attempt has been made recently to calculate various theoretical figures for the quantity of material needed (see Bibliography), including the suggestion that the entire system would have needed in the region of 3.7 million tonnes of stone. That the Wall functioned as a completed entity is an assumption usually made. It may be right, but not necessarily so. We have no evidence that the Wall was finished throughout its length though this is not the same as proof that it was not. But the paucity of evidence for its superstructure, coupled with other instances of apparently uncompleted military buildings (such as at Birdoswald) and protracted phases of decay, along with a commonsense appraisal of other massive engineering projects compromised by time and altered circumstances, makes it a possibility which should not be discounted.

Purpose, strategy and tactics

The Wall had no one purpose. The system must have provided a psychological boost to the population further south. Likewise it would have appeared as a potent statement to those in its vicinity and beyond. It may have served as a practical project for the army to be involved in to toughen them up. Acting as an absolute barrier was clearly not part of the scheme because outpost forts beyond the Wall, for example at Bewcastle and Birrens, indicate that Rome regarded land immediately to the north as under her control. In any case a determined raider would have had little difficulty in scaling the Wall if he so desired.

The Wall and its various crossing points made it possible to supervise local movements, just in the way a modern border channels traffic. The difference between the vista presented by the Wall and ditch to the north, and the Vallum to the south, may suggest a more sophisticated and even seasonal policy of control. It is possible, for instance, that access to the province from the north was devised to let individuals or groups in under supervision to trade or even seek seasonal agricultural work, but who were then obliged to pass along the Vallum zone to enter the province elsewhere, perhaps having been broken up into smaller parties. When they attempted to leave the province they could enter the Vallum zone relatively easily but were then corralled, searched and taxed; perhaps they were then moved along east or west to leave the province elsewhere along the Wall in dispersed groups away from anywhere that was showing signs of unrest.

The turrets and milecastles could only have been designed to make observations and communications easy, and to control small-scale movements. As a small matter of interest, it takes approximately $2\frac{1}{2}$ minutes to run between a pair of turrets. The garrisons of projecting forts, like Benwell and Chesters, usually included cavalry; their plans could have allowed rapid dispersal north of the fort and Wall. This traditional interpretation is complicated by the fact that some of their gates on the north side of the Wall were blocked up partly or completely shortly after construction and by the re-alignment of the Wall at Birdoswald to bring the whole fort south, suggesting that any such tactic was swiftly abandoned.

Even with the forts a theoretical Wall garrison of something like 8–10,000 men was distributed along the whole length, of which at any time probably no more than a half to two-thirds were actually available for a variety of reasons. Consequently the number of men available in any given area was limited to a few hundred. If this was effective, and it certainly never materially altered, then it seems that the scheme was designed as more of a policing presence than offensive warfare.

In time the Wall probably became so integrated a part of military routine and local civilian life that its original intentions were largely forgotten. It is the kind of ancient structure that invokes modern incredulity, particularly with regard to cost. But Hadrian's Wall cost nothing at all. The materials were free and the soldiers were being paid regardless. This makes it easier to understand how Hadrian's Wall could have been built in the first place, and temporarily abandoned 20 years after it was built.

THE LATER SECOND CENTURY

The Antonine Wall and the abandonment of Hadrian's Wall
The Antonine Wall runs between the Forth and Clyde in Scotland, about 100 miles (160km) north of Hadrian's Wall. It was built under the orders of Antoninus Pius in the early 140s, and was permanently abandoned in the 160s. His Roman biographer states that he built a turf wall in Britain once the governor, Lollius Urbicus, had defeated the 'barbarians' (Source 9). Pius may have needed to establish a reputation for himself as a firm ruler but perhaps there were local problems like idle soldiers and difficulties with supplying the remote central sector forts. There may even have been a change of policy requiring more exact control of the area north of Hadrian's Wall, perhaps connected with the fact that the latter cut across the tribal lands of the Brigantes, the principal tribe of northern Britain. The plan may even have been to create a kind of 'neutral zone' between the Walls through which individuals and groups could pass.

The new frontier was only 37 Roman miles (59km) long, or around half that of Hadrian's Wall. It was modelled on its predecessor but was built entirely of turf on a cobble base 14 Roman feet (4.1m) wide. The new frontier had a forward ditch, about 20–30 Roman feet (6–9m) wide, but no equivalent to the Vallum was ever dug. Unlike Hadrian's Wall the forts were designed to be part of the new frontier from the beginning, and even preceded the turf curtain in some cases; however a second wave of forts seem to have been added during construction. The forts were interspersed with fortlets but there is no positive evidence for a regular series of turrets. Their combined capacity means that the total garrison cannot have been very much less than that on Hadrian's Wall. In military terms this supplied twice as many men per mile of frontier than before. The new frontier was backed up by the garrisoning of forts in the land between the Walls. At High Rochester, an old Flavian fort site was utilized to create a new stone fort. At Birrens, the Hadrianic fort seems to have remained in occupation, with rebuilding work apparently undertaken by detachments of Rhine legions (Source 9).

Controlled movement across Hadrian's Wall is thought to have been abandoned: the milecastle gates were either removed or left open, and crossings were installed on the Vallum (the latter remain the clearest trace of this policy today, but are not easily datable). As far as the forts are concerned their garrisons were probably transferred to the new Wall. Unfortunately, so few early garrisons on Hadrian's Wall are known that this is difficult to demonstrate but the First Cohort of Hamian archers, stationed at the Stanegate fort of Carvoran under Hadrian, was posted to Bar Hill on the Antonine Wall for a while before returning to Carvoran (Source 7). Even so, it is unlikely that the Hadrian's Wall forts were abandoned. There is a very small amount of evidence to suggest that some of the forts were occupied by legionaries; for example, an incomplete legionary dedicatory inscription from Chesters names Antoninus Pius and gives enough detail to say that it dates to somewhere in the period 139–61. At Benwell an altar from the temple of Antenociticus, near the fort, names a legionary of the II Legion for the same period. At Birdoswald there is no discernible gap in datable finds of the second century. However, some parts of the fort, unbuilt on since its construction, remained open; as these included the site of the later granaries it has been suggested that the fort was only manned by a reduced garrison.

It's unfortunate that we know so little about the history of later Roman Britain. Most of our detailed historical information dates to the first century, such as the accounts written by Tacitus. Thereafter historians and archaeologists have no choice but to piece together a chronology from brief literary references to Britain, inscriptions, coin issues which refer to events in Britain, and archaeology. Even this deteriorates because inscriptions, never common, become even scarcer after the early third century, and literary references increasingly sporadic and more unreliable. So it has proved difficult to avoid making much from little. This is far from unusual in archaeology, even for the Roman period. Britain was a backwater, a testing ground for premier military careers, but otherwise of only secondary importance to the Empire. She became useful and productive but was always of marginal importance, making headline news in Rome only when war broke out. This forces a reliance on what is recovered from the ground. But, there is no avoiding the reality that pottery and coin evidence is far too imprecise, however carefully researched, to provide exact chronologies when historical references and inscriptions are lacking.

In the period 142–4, around the same time as the Antonine Wall was begun, coins were struck depicting Britannia, and were followed by a similar issue (which is normally only found in Britain) for the years 154–5 (**10**). Such coins were usually produced at times of military success but they do not always explicitly state this. The geographer Pausanias describes a phase of warfare

*10   Coins of Antoninus Pius. **a**.* Sestertius *of 142–4 showing Britannia. **b**.* As *of 154–5 showing Britannia in defeated pose. The latter was circulated almost exclusively in Britain.*

during Pius' reign which may have taken place in northern Britain, but he appears to have been mistaken or had confused two different wars (Source 10). The arrival of legionary reinforcements at Newcastle from Germany or the return of detachments temporarily sent to Germany (**17**; Source 11), and rebuilding at Birrens (Source 10), about this time might suggest something was afoot. Destruction and repair on the Antonine Wall may be attributable to these implicit phases of warfare.

But archaeologists have no doubt that the Antonine Wall saw two distinct phases of occupation, following careful examination of two levels of destruction and demolition debris. The problems are when and for how long, and whether the phases ended because of defeat or deliberate withdrawal. These have proved difficult to resolve.

The reoccupation of Hadrian's Wall

Hadrian's Wall was recommissioned by the 160s, though repair work is testified by 158 (Source 11). Calpurnius Agricola was sent to govern Britain around 163. He is mentioned by the biographer of Marcus Aurelius (Source 12) and his name appears on inscriptions at Carvoran and Stanwix (Sources 13 and 14). It seems reasonable to assume that the Antonine Wall had, by then, been given up for good. If there was any Turf Wall left in the western sector of Hadrian's Wall it was now replaced in stone. Some of the turrets were

11   Sestertius *of Commodus (180–92), reverse only, dated to the year 184 with the legend* VICT BRIT *for* Victoria Britannica.

demolished between this period and c.220, being reduced to their lower courses and the Wall restored to full width over them. It is unlikely that the Walls were occupied simultaneously. So, a logical assumption would be that somewhere between the late 150s and early 170s a decision was made to give up the Antonine Wall. The forts to its rear, such as High Rochester, remained in use, showing that withdrawal did not mean that the Roman command regarded the area beyond Hadrian's Wall as abandoned. The visible fort at South Shields seems to belong to this period, reinforcing control of the lower reaches of the river Tyne to the east of the end of the Wall at Wallsend.

The Roman army retained a precarious hold on northern Britain. Cassius Dio, describing the reign of Commodus (180–92), mentions a war in Britain which he said was the most troublesome of the reign (Source 15). Damage at some forts, such as Haltonchesters, has been attributed to this event, but only on the loosest circumstantial association. Dio states that a wall was involved but does not specify which or even if it was manned (though he makes clear he means just one), so we can only assume that he was referring to Hadrian's Wall while appreciating that he might have meant a crossing of the abandoned Antonine Wall. Whatever happened, the tribes were apparently suppressed because in 184 coins were issued with legends stating explicitly 'Vict[oria] Brit[annica]' (**11**).

THE THIRD CENTURY AND BEYOND

Septimius Severus

During the Roman civil war of the mid-190s Britain's governor Clodius Albinus used the province's garrison to support his claim to the throne. He was defeated by Septimius Severus in 197 at a battle in Gaul near Lyons. Whether this had involved Wall troops is no more than likely, and what the consequences had been to the Wall structures can only be surmised. If Albinus had withdrawn Wall troops this might explain the extensive rebuilding work which followed under Septimius Severus, either as a result of decay or attacks from tribes.

Towards the end of his reign Severus undertook a campaign into Scotland to concentrate the minds of his decadent sons Caracalla and Geta. A number of Wall forts have yielded inscriptions from the early third century showing that individual buildings were repaired or restored; similar renovation of the curtain (much of it rebuilt on an even more reduced width of about 6.5ft, or 1.9m), using a distinctive hard white mortar, the demolition of some turrets, and the narrowing of some milecastle gates may belong to this phase. But, what looks from our point of view like a tight scattering of examples of repair work in reality spread across a generation. One of the most explicit, from the fort at Birdoswald, records repairs in 205–8 to a granary (Source 18). Despite the theoretical historical background it is inevitable that structures around a century old might need substantial rebuilding, thanks to rotted roof timbers, uneven settling of foundations and general decay.

The Peel Gap tower was apparently demolished somewhere around this time (its pottery sequence does not go beyond the early third century) and the Wall rebuilt over its remains and those of the earlier curtain. This kind of work was probably done as required, and was in part a consequence of the peaceful state that prevailed after Severus' campaigns. Contemporary historians are silent; things were so quiet that the forts seem quietly to have fallen down again. At Birdoswald an inscription of 297–305 records that several buildings were ruined and covered in earth, and had to be rebuilt (Source 21). As they included the headquarters building, the commandant's house, and the bath-house(?), the fort must have spent a long time in which its existence was of no value at all. It should be added that there is a school of thought which considers these references to 'decay' as euphemisms for barbarian destruction. Following this line, however, makes it possible to 'interpret' every inscription exactly as one pleases. Ultimately we have to take much of what we have with guarded trust – the explicitness of the Birdoswald stone and the lack of evidence for violent destruction makes it more likely that we are dealing with an approximation of the truth.

Carausius and Allectus

If Birdoswald had been allowed to decay for many years then other forts on the Wall may have suffered similar neglect; a fragmentary inscription from

Housesteads of similar date might record building work there too (Source 21). But the repairs require an explanation. By the end of the third century the Empire was ruled by two senior emperors, Diocletian and Maximianus, who governed the east and west respectively with their assistants Galerius and Constantius Chlorus – the so-called Tetrarchy. In 286 the commander of the British fleet, Carausius, had set himself up as an independent emperor in Britain. He was remarkably successful, and apparently popular, but had not reckoned with the duplicity of his associate Allectus who had him murdered in 293. Allectus then ruled, only to be defeated and killed in 296 by Constantius' army at a battle in southern Britain.

Perhaps the decay and damage found on Wall sites is attributable to Carausius or Allectus withdrawing Wall troops to bolster resistance against the Tetrarchy, and thus exposing the Wall to cross-border raiding by northern tribes. It's quite plausible, but not demonstrable. The Birdoswald inscription of 297–305 describes natural decay there so it may be that the repairs on the Wall forts simply came about during another phase of renovation. Some barrack blocks were comprehensively redesigned: the contiguous strips of rooms were replaced by rows of individual chambers identified at Housesteads and Wallsend. Alterations at milecastles, such as gate sizes, or the new gate through the Wall by the Knag Burn near Housesteads, are only some examples of numerous changes. They serve to show that much of the Wall system was functioning and being maintained. That some forts like Haltonchesters have shown no evidence (yet) for repair indicates that restoration was unnecessary either because the fort was largely redundant or was in too good a state of repair to need it.

It's sobering to consider how much time had passed by now since the Wall had been built. The soldiers who had built the Wall were as remote to the fourth-century garrison of the Wall as the army and navy of George III during the Napoleonic Wars are to us. In such a context it is easier to understand why there should have been protracted phases of rebuilding, decay, and alterations in purpose.

Fourth-century change and reconstruction

Occasional literary references to Britain suggest that the northern frontier was a cause of official concern and military activity in the years 306, 346, and 360. Then the historian Ammianus Marcellinus recorded that a barbarian conspiracy plunged Britain into what he called 'a state of helpless despair' in 367 (Source 22). The emperor Valentinian sent the general Theodosius to deal with the situation. Unfortunately, these sources are vague about what was going on. Ammianus suggests there was widespread anarchy, but Theodosius re-established control, 'renewed the cities and forts of the provincial garrison', and put guards on the frontiers. We might reasonably assume that Hadrian's Wall had been affected. However, there is no evidence of any destruction on the Wall at around this time – perhaps the raiders avoided wasting time in burning Wall forts and made their way south. Wall repair work is recorded on

12   *Centurial stone from milecastle 42 at Cawfields recording the presence of unit of wall-builders sent by the local goverment of the Durotriges tribal area in south-western Britain. Probably fourth century.*

a few inscribed stones, normally attributed to the fourth century on the basis of style. Some of these name peoples of southern Britain, such as the Durotriges (**12**), suggesting a province-wide organized programme of defensive renewal which would certainly fit in with what we know about Theodosius. The outpost forts have not yet produced evidence for sustained occupation into the late fourth century, so they were probably not part of the new scheme and may have been abandoned.

This brings us close to the end of Roman Britain. The *Notitia Dignitatum* shows that, officially at any rate, the forts were manned from one end to the other (Source 22). Of course it could have been drawn up from obsolete information, but the absence of the outpost forts from the list, thought to have been given up by the late 360s, suggests it was not very out-of-date.

THE END

Within fifty years Britain had drifted into the twilight of what we call the Dark Ages. We can never fathom what happened because most of evidence we rely on ceased to exist. It was once assumed that the absence of Roman coins and pottery meant an absence of people. All it actually means is that pottery and coins gradually ceased to be used; the process was gradual, but certainly not protracted. No new coins entered Britain from soon after the beginning of the fifth century, and the shortfall was not made good in Britain as it had been on those occasions when supplies were interrupted before. By about 430 life had changed forever. But meticulous excavation, of the type conducted at Birdoswald in recent years, can sometimes show that, *after* the datable evidence runs out, structures continued in use, had time to fall down and then be replaced with new buildings. In this way the history of Birdoswald has been extended by a theoretical (but no more than) further century.

Birdoswald has revealed that an organized and centralized community probably continued to exist here, or perhaps just subsist, after the Roman period. One old granary was adapted to serve as a kind of hall, while the site of another granary, immediately adjacent, had been used for another timber building. This may have taken place in the late fourth or the fifth century, but there is practically no certain datable evidence for activity here until the thirteenth century, nearly a thousand years later. What happened at Birdoswald may have happened elsewhere. Happily, some of the forts on the Wall survive practically untouched by archaeologists or anyone else, so the possibility remains that they will yield more information in the future.

The fifth-century and later occupants of Birdoswald probably traced their ancestral and cultural origins back to the Roman military units. The discovery of their presence has shown that the remnants of Hadrian's Wall were substantial and significant features in the history of the area for much longer than previously realized. A tombstone from Vindolanda (now at Chesters) names 'Brigomaglos' and uses Latin in a form which has more to do with early Christian society than Roman. Undatable, it probably belongs to some time in the fifth or sixth century.

In the end the forts and the Wall ceased to have a cohesive military and political definition. Once they had marked the frontier of the Roman Empire; now they became a resource. Where convenient a fort might serve as a fortified farmstead, the milecastles as occasional sheep corrals or, along with the curtain, as handy quarries. In this way the Wall served the local inhabitants handsomely for centuries and would continue to do so were it not for our heritage-conscious age.

THE ARMY ON THE WALL

The Roman army of the second century AD was made up of the citizen legionaries and the non-citizen auxiliaries. The legionaries served in 5000-strong legions and were a combination of first-rate infantry and the modern British Army's Royal Engineers. They built and administered the military infrastructure of forts, roads, and frontiers. Britain had three legions in the 120s: II *Augusta*, XX *Valeria Victrix*, and VI *Victrix*. The latter was a very recent arrival and probably accompanied Hadrian from Germany, replacing IX *Hispana* which seems to have been transferred elsewhere. Their inscriptions record their building activity; but, an example of mid-second-century date from the outpost fort at Birrens naming VIII *Augusta* and XXII *Primigenia*, shows that detachments from other legions were occasionally brought in to help (Source 9). Dedications elsewhere show that legionary personnel had an intermittent presence on the Wall, and fought in the area, but they did not provide the garrisons. After the middle of the second century a commander of the VI Legion, one Lucius Junius Victorinus, dedicated an altar found west of Carlisle at Kirksteads on which he commemorated successful exploits *trans vallum* ('across the Wall'; Source 17).

The rest of the army were the *auxilia*, units of infantry, cavalry, or a mixture. Recruited originally from around the Empire they retained their ethnic names even if they enlisted new troops from where they were stationed and no longer bore any real resemblance to the original units. They served as the primary frontier garrisons and were the first to challenge the enemy on the battlefield. They were not normally posted to their nominal homelands. They were less well paid than legionaries and had to serve 25 years to earn an honourable discharge and citizenship. We now know from the written evidence, surviving at Vindolanda in Britain (discussed below) and Dura-Europos in Syria, that the nominal sizes of these units are just figures of convenience which have been taken far too literally in the past.

In the auxiliary infantry regiments a *cohors peditata quingenaria* (literally 'an infantry cohort consisting of 500') was what we might call a 'small cohort' of infantry at a nominal 500 strength. In fact, it was made up of six 'centuries' of 80 men not including officers. A 'large cohort' was called a *cohors peditata millaria* but instead of being 1000 strong it was made up of ten centuries of 80 men, making a milliary cohort of 800.

In the auxiliary cavalry regiments an *ala quingenaria* was a 'small wing' of cavalry of nominal 500 strength but this time made up of 16 *turmae* of 32 men each, making 512 not including officers. A 'large wing' was called an *ala millaria* and had 24 *turmae*, making 768 men. Britain, like all provinces, had only one such unit, the Ala Petriana, stationed at Stanwix, the largest fort on the Wall. It is likely that this was where the Wall system was administered from though the military high command of all northern Britain was the headquarters of the VI Legion at York. After c.215 that Legion's commander was governor of the province of Britannia Inferior (Source 25).

Auxiliary units were also created out of a combination of infantry and cavalry. This was simply achieved by adding four *turmae*, or 128 men, to a 'small cohort' which thus ended up with 608 men and was called a *cohors equitata quingenaria* (literally 'a mounted cohort consisting of 500'). Eight *turmae* added to a 'large cohort' created a unit of 800 foot and 256 cavalry or 1056 men, and was called a *cohors equitata millaria*.

Whether or not these fort-based auxiliary units provided the manpower for the milecastles and turrets, perhaps on a rotation basis, is completely unknown. It is possible that detachments for these duties were provided by Stanegate fort garrisons. Unfortunately finds from these sites are sparse, making it extremely difficult to draw firm conclusions about their garrisons. A reused tombstone at milecastle 42 (Cawfields), bearing the name of a unit not testified at a Wall fort, suggests that turret and milecastle troops might have been drawn from almost anywhere suitable.

The evidence for auxiliary unit administration is correspondingly sparse. Their names come from inscriptions on altars, dedication slabs, and the *Notitia Dignitatum*. Roman authors certainly did not elaborate in detail which implies that the detail was not of great significance, at any rate to them. Unit strengths probably varied according to circumstance. Evidence from diplomas (see Glossary), and the Vindolanda writing tablets, shows that units were not only moved around the Empire at short notice, but were also sometimes broken up into detachments posted at several different locations. So, the old picture of a relatively fixed system of garrisons, based on inscriptions, has proved to be rather false. We can only glimpse snapshots. For example, a diploma dated 17 July 122 (Sources 6 and 25) states that on that day Britain had 37 auxiliary cohorts of infantry. Five years later, on 20 August 127, that number had dropped to 27 thanks to transfers. The same diplomas say that in 122 there were 13 cavalry units, but only eight in 127.

An establishment report of mid-May in c.90–100 survives from waterlogged levels at Vindolanda. Itemising 752 men of the First Cohort of Tungrians under the command of Julius Verecundus, the report reveals that 337 were on duties at the nearby fort of Corbridge, 46 were on the provincial governor's guard duty, and various others were scattered elsewhere. Only 296 were left at Vindolanda (including only one centurion), of whom 31 were sick or wounded. So, in this case at least, a 752-strong cohort was no more precise a term than our 'hundred yards' and suggests that discussions about the garrison on the Wall have been rather academic in the past. Just as the Wall and its specifications turn out to be only nominal, so the same was true of the Roman army.

The legions which built the Wall system were occasionally assisted by auxiliaries and the *Classis Britannica* (the British arm of the Roman fleet; Source 3). Thereafter, the frontier was manned by the auxiliaries, who also seem to have engaged in repair, rebuilding, and maintenance work in later centuries. The different types and sizes of unit were variously dispersed along the Wall. We know the names of very few in the Hadrianic period but more from later on. Sometimes they were moved about but by the third century most appear to have been settled, with troops marrying local women and producing hybrid self-sustaining communities.

By the later second century some of the forts had attracted civilian settlement. Such settlements (*vici*) have been found across the Roman Empire, though compared to the prominent military fortifications they are distinguished by random and straggling development. Some auxiliary soldiers undoubtedly raised families, albeit unrecognized in Roman law, and this laid the foundation for future recruitment and community involvement in the unit. They brought with them their own gods as well, dedicating altars and shrines as individuals and as members of their units. All along the Wall evidence has been found for cults of local water nymphs, obscure warrior gods, official gods, and many others such as the eastern god Mithras. The Roman fort emerges as just the focus of a whole complex human settlement. Like miniature Woolwich Arsenals every fort and its community would have been characterized by local circumstances, and vice-versa.

By the middle of the second century a number of 'inferior' forms of auxiliary unit start appearing in Britain. These were more casually organized, less well-paid, and did not earn citizenship on retirement. An infantry unit was called a *numerus*. This means what it looks like: a 'number' or 'body' of troops. However, the testified existence of cavalry officers, decurions, in some *numeri* suggests they may have had a cavalry component when necessary. A cavalry unit was a *cuneus*, literally a 'wedge' or 'wedge-shaped formation'. Finally there were the *exploratores*, or 'scouts', and *venatores*, or 'hunters'. By the fourth century the movement of auxiliary troops had really long since ceased. Units remained where they were, and official records described them rather disparagingly as *limitanei*, just frontier guards, to contrast them with the higher status field armies.

THE SURVIVING REMAINS

While Hadrian's army in Britain was responsible for building the Wall in its primary state, very little of what can be seen today is demonstrably Hadrianic. Only the recovery of Hadrianic building stones here and there has proved building work of that period. Much of the curtain and many of the forts were subjected to major repair and reconstruction during the Roman period, sometimes within little more than a generation after the Wall was begun. After the Roman period the systematic destruction of long sections of Wall proceeded apace as the stones were taken away to be used for buildings elsewhere. The significant expansion of towns and settlements in the nineteenth century was responsible for an increase in the rate of destruction. As a result in our own time Hadrian's Wall, as a recognizable fortification, is largely confined to the central upland sector between Chesters and Birdoswald and much of that is either late-Roman rebuilding or even modern restoration.

2. Wallsend to Chesters

The Wall system begins in the outskirts of Newcastle upon Tyne. A car or bicycle is fine for reaching Wallsend but the area is well served by public transport. Newcastle city centre, in particular, should be avoided by motorists. The Metro system is excellent and is one of the best ways to reach the Museum of Antiquities, as well as Wallsend fort.

13　　*The remains of the headquarters building at Wallsend as consolidated. The view is south-east across the western colonnade, the courtyard and beyond the forehall. The Wall ran down from the south-eastern corner of the fort into the Tyne approximately on the site of the large shed at upper left.*

14   *Reconstructed stretch of Hadrian's Wall outside the north-west corner of the fort at Wallsend.*

WALLSEND (*Segedunum*)

★★Visible remains★★: *complete fort platform overlooked by the new museum and observation tower, replica bath-house, and replica stretch of Wall (across Buddle Street). Entrance charge. Open all year round (10-5 summer, 10-3.30 winter, closed). Tel: 0191 236 9347. Parking by the museum or a 200m walk south from Wallsend Metro Station down Station Road, or from the bus station down Carville Road. A–Z map Site p. 47 D4, Metro D3. OS Ref. NZ 300660 (Sheet 88 1:50 000 Series).*

The first visible portion of Wall is the stretch attached to the south-east corner of Wallsend fort by the Swan Hunter shipyard. It joined the 4 acre (1.6ha) fort to the river Tyne and was visible in early modern times but industrial development has long since destroyed all but a tiny fragment. Building also extended over the fort itself but the site has now been cleared. Fragments of the fortifications, gates, and the headquarters building were consolidated and left on public display, following a series of excavations between 1975–84 (**13**). These produced the most complete plan (albeit partly conjectural) of any fort on the Wall system. Unfortunately, the site subsequently became rather run down but, thanks to a National Lottery award, the fort is now being re-excavated. When the work is finished a new museum and far more of the site will be open to the public.

Difficult to find without a road map, Wallsend fort is now bisected by Buddle Street (the A186/187). The re-excavation of the site means that visible

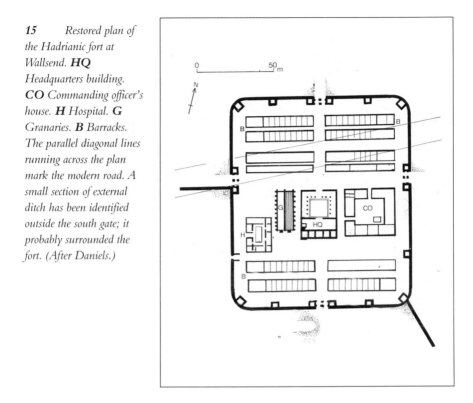

15 *Restored plan of the Hadrianic fort at Wallsend.* **HQ** *Headquarters building.* **CO** *Commanding officer's house.* **H** *Hospital.* **G** *Granaries.* **B** *Barracks. The parallel diagonal lines running across the plan mark the modern road. A small section of external ditch has been identified outside the south gate; it probably surrounded the fort. (After Daniels.)*

remains are in flux and may not be accessible. Nevertheless, a short stretch of replica Wall has been built alongside the foundations of the real Wall outside the north-west corner of the fort on the north side of Buddle Street. With a walkway and parapet, this is just one possible way to restore the Wall but the replica is a vivid piece of work and it is the only example along the whole length of the Wall at present (**14**).

Considering its past, it is fortunate that *Segedunum* ('victory fort') is visible at all. Like most of northern England this area was largely rural until the Industrial Revolution when, in 1778, mining began here. Before long, the fort had been covered with mine buildings and miners' houses. Subsequently shipbuilding, centred on the Swan Hunter yards, became a major source of employment. The fort remained largely buried but parts were visible. In 1885 Collingwood Bruce recorded that the previous year he had been able to find 'some slight traces', including the 'grass-grown mound of the eastern rampart'. Local people told him that the Wall was once visible 'extending far into the stream' from the south-east corner of the fort. Bruce feared for the fort's future, writing that 'the whole of the ground occupied by the camp is being laid out as building ground'. Of course no-one then could have anticipated the prospects for heavy industry, the decline of which made way for large-scale clearance and demolition in Wallsend, incidentally creating the opportunity to re-expose the fort.

16 *Portable lead shrine from Wallsend showing the god Mercury and elements associated with other gods. It had a pair of doors and was thus probably a 'pocket' version of a household shrine. Fourth century. Height 75mm.*

The fort site was well chosen. It occupies a small plateau overlooking the Tyne to the south, and commands wide views east and west across the valley. The fort had four main gates, and one additional minor one in the western rampart. More of the fort projected north of the Wall than at any other fort, thanks to its orientation (**15**). Excavation in 1929 revealed that the west gate, and the curtain which abuts it, were of one build. The other forts can normally be shown to have been later additions to the Wall. But, the Wall from here to Newcastle is entirely Narrow gauge, including the foundations, so it seems reasonable to suppose that Wallsend fort *and* the Wall here were an afterthought. Perhaps it had not been considered essential to control access from the north to the riverbank of the Tyne east of the Roman bridge at Newcastle.

The restored plan of the fort (**15**) shows that in its earliest, Hadrianic, phase the fort contained the usual structures of central headquarters building (**13**), a commandant's house, granaries, and barracks. Another structure, of uncertain identity, may have been the hospital. Bruce recorded that an inscription naming the II Legion was found here, and so perhaps had built the fort. In the third century the headquarters building and adjacent granaries seem to have been joined together by walls and a forehall, perhaps serving as a covered parade ground.

Oddly, none of the Wallsend gates showed signs of having been blocked up, something which seems to have happened almost everywhere else on the Wall forts. However, the replacement of the barracks by individual chambers in the fourth century is matched elsewhere, for example at Housesteads. The only unit which was certainly stationed here was the Fourth mounted Cohort of Lingones. Recorded on altars of late style, it was probably here in the third and fourth centuries. A small lead shrine, depicting Mercury, may have belonged to one of them (**16**). The Second Cohort of Nervians visited at some date and dedicated a relief of Mercury, so it seems likely that there was a shrine to the god at Wallsend. It may have been that built by a centurion called Gaius Julius Maximinus from the VI Legion. He recorded the fact on a stone which probably came from here.

Depending on individual itineraries, either head west for Newcastle following the rest of this chapter, or head east on the A187 for the Tyne Tunnel to visit South Shields (see Chapter 8). Nothing of the Wall system can be seen to the west of Wallsend for several miles. If driving, head towards Newcastle on the A187, joining the A193 at Byker. Sporadic excavations and building work have uncovered traces here and there under the sprawl of Newcastle and its suburbs, for example the south-west corner of a milecastle off Westgate Road, west of central Newcastle at NZ 245640. Some way from the theoretical placing of either milecastle 4 or 5, this example shows how much the Wall and its remains can vary from expectations.

NEWCASTLE

Visible remains: *plans of some internal buildings of the fort marked with modern stonework in the grounds of the Norman castle. Accessible on foot from Metro Central Station – head east down Neville Street into Westgate Road where it meets St Nicholas Street. A–Z map Site p. 143 D5, Metro C5. OS Ref. NZ 300660 (Sheet 88 1:50 000 Series).*

A fort, called *Pons Aelius*, stood at Newcastle in the fourth century and is listed in the *Notitia Dignitatum* as being manned by the First Cohort of Cornovians (a British tribe, whose region was centred on Wroxeter near modern Shrewsbury – an unusual instance of an auxiliary unit serving in its own province). In 213 the First Cohort of Roman-citizen Cubernians was the garrison here, testified on a recently-found inscription. However, it was only a few years ago that some of the fort buildings were identified in the grounds of the Norman castle. Modern stonework in the pavement on the north and west side of the castle, running under the arches of the railway viaduct, marks the buried remains of the sites of the headquarters building, the commanding officer's house, and a granary.

The fort's name comes from the bridge across the Tyne. Aelius was one of Hadrian's names and therefore the bridge must have been built during his reign. It was certainly there by the 150s (see below). Little is known about the

17   *Inscription from the Tyne at Newcastle recording legionary movements in c. 155–9. For a discussion of its exact meaning see Source 11. Width 0.66m. (Photo: author, used with permission of Museum of Antiquities, Newcastle.)*

bridge other than that it had stone piers and may have survived in use up to the medieval period. Later bridges utilized the foundations which were identified in the mid-nineteenth century. Many of the remarkable finds dredged from the riverbed are displayed in the Museum of Antiquities in Newcastle.

THE MUSEUM OF ANTIQUITIES

Open all year round Monday to Saturday 10.00–5.00. Free. Tel: 0191–222–7846. At the University of Newcastle. Access by car not recommended but there are public car-parks in the vicinity (e.g. in Claremont Road, just off the A167, and 5-minutes walk from the museum). Easiest access is from the Haymarket Metro stop 200m to the east. Head south down Percy Street, taking a right turn (west) up Saint Thomas Street, and then right again (north) up Kings Road through the middle of the University. Turn left through an arch just beneath a bridge over the road and the entrance to the museum is just round the corner to the left. A–Z Map p. 142 C2 (Claremont Road car-park p.142 B1).

The Museum of Antiquities has many of the finest monuments found along the Wall. Most of these are stone carvings and inscriptions. One of the most striking records the arrival of reinforcements to the legions in Britain in the late 150s during the reign of Antoninus Pius (**17**; Source 11). The stone is well-preserved because it was dredged from the river near the site of the Roman

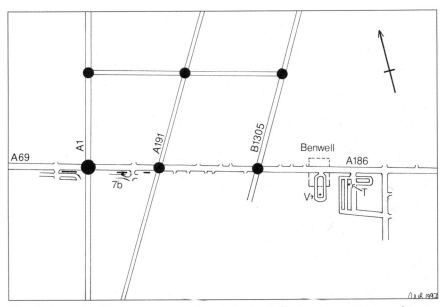

Map 2 *Benwell to Denton Burn, approximately 2 miles (3.2km) east to west (not to scale).*
T★ = Benwell Temple of Antenociticus in Broomridge Avenue. V★ = Benwell Vallum crossing
in Denhill Park. **7b** *= Turret 7b (Denton Burn). Other sections of Wall are shown as bold lines*
to the south of the east-west road.

bridge in Newcastle. Other stones include dedication slabs from milecastles
and forts which make the building of the Wall by Hadrian a certainty (for
example, Sources 2 and 3). Stones are also on display from sites along the Wall
which no longer have any visible remains, such as the Temple of Mithras at the
fort of Rudchester. There is a fascinating scale model of the whole Wall which
runs down the middle of the museum hall. Visitors should also make sure they
see the reconstructed interior of the mithraeum (temple of Mithras), based on
the remains at the fort of Carrawburgh.

From Newcastle the motorist should leave by the A186 (West Road), which
runs on the course of the Wall, and make for Benwell. This involves entering
the one-way system first, heading along Neville Street in front of the station,
until signposted right (north), and then left (west) for the A186 to head out for
Benwell.

BENWELL (*Condercum*)

★★*Visible remains*★★: *temple and Vallum (Map 2). English Heritage. Free. Temple in
Broomridge Avenue via Weidner Road off West Road (A186, but also labelled A6115 in
some older maps), and Vallum in Denhill Park (next turning). The Metro does not reach
out here. A–Z Map p. 58: temple C2, Vallum B1. OS Ref. NZ 215646 (Sheet 88 1:
50 000 Series).*

18   *The temple of Antenociticus, south-west of the fort at Benwell. The two altars are modern reproductions (the originals are at Newcastle). The view is from the south-east.*

Nothing is visible of any of the Wall from Wallsend until Benwell. The fort here stood on a prominent hill about 2.5 miles (4km) to the west of modern central Newcastle. The Roman name *Condercum* is highly appropriate for it means something like 'good views in all directions', based on the Celtic words *com* 'with' and *derco*, 'looking around'. None of the actual fort can now be seen at all for a reservoir has long since covered the section north of the road (and thus north of the Wall), and what remained was covered by a housing estate before the Second World War.

Benwell was built to oversee the Denton Burn stream to the west which flows into the Tyne. The fort projected north of the Wall which, together with its size of 5.6 acres (2.2ha), suggests it was to be manned by a part-mounted unit. An inscription records that a unit from the Roman fleet in Britain was sent here to build the granaries under Hadrian (Source 3). Why the fleet should have been involved is a mystery but perhaps there was an element of urgency about the project and all available manpower was brought in.

The remains here consist of the footings of a small temple to a little-known Celtic god called Antenociticus or Anociticus (**18**), and those of a crossing over the Vallum to the south of the fort (**6**) (Map 2). Neither is indicated from the main road and signposts in the minor roads are usually pointed in the wrong directions. The temple can be reached by turning left from the A186 just past a garage into Weidner Road which is opposite West Gate Community College (formerly a school, and marked as such on maps). Once in Weidner Road turn

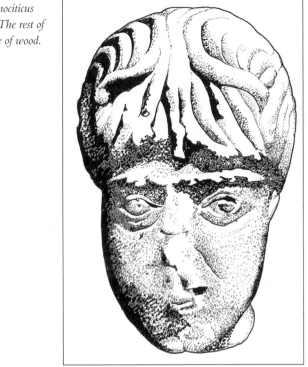

19   Stone head of Antenociticus from the temple at Benwell. The rest of the statue was probably made of wood. Life size.

immediately right and then sharp left into Broomridge Avenue. The temple lies a few yards down the hill on the left-hand side of the road in an open plot between modern houses opposite numbers 45 and 47.

When the temple was excavated the stone head of the god (**19**) was found along with three altars, all of which named him. The visible altars are casts (the originals, and the head of the god, are at Newcastle). They record the names of Aelius Vibius, a centurion of the XX Legion, and Tineius Longus, 'prefect of cavalry'. The Longus altar gives the names of the governor Ulpius Marcellus and is dated to 177–80 (Sources 15 and 16). The unit stationed at Benwell, of which Longus was probably commander, the First Cohort of Vangiones, is named on the third (broken) altar. The temple was a tiny building with an internal area of only about 15 square metres. It's a simple rectangle with apse, and an entrance in one side.

When the Vallum was built it skirted most of the Wall forts to the south as here. At Benwell (and probably at the other forts) a crossing was installed with a substantial masonry gateway (**6**). The foundations of this gate and a section of Vallum can be seen in Denhill Park, the next turning off the A186 after Weidner Road (but not accessible from the latter – return to the main road and head a few metres west). Turn left into Denhill Park and take the left fork. The road runs down the hill across the fort and then turns right past the exposed Vallum crossing.

45

The remains can be seen through an iron fence. A local key is (or was) available, but in May 1997 there was no information about access. A small section of Vallum has been consolidated to illustrate its neat profile of slanting sides and broad flat base, though the original depth was about twice what can be seen here today. The crossing, approached from north and south by the remains of the metalled Roman road, was created with a revetted stone filling, topped by a substantial masonry gate. Of the latter only the lowest blocks remain but their form suggests a symmetrical and imposing stone arch, with timber gates. Curiously, despite Benwell's present state, this is the only extant example of a monumental Vallum crossing. About 55m to the north lay the south gate of the fort. To leave here carry on round the road and turn left (west) back on to the A186.

DENTON BURN

★★Visible remains★★: *19m stretch of Wall in fenced enclosure in front of Charlie Brown's garage forecourt just west of Denton Road (A191) (Map 2). OS Ref. NZ 202654 (Sheet 88 1: 50 000 Series).*

If this stretch of Wall was anywhere else it would not be mentioned, but apart from the short pieces at Wallsend this is the first stretch which can be seen. Unlike the Wallsend fragments it was built on Broad Wall measurements from the beginning. Unfortunately, it has little else to recommend it; only four courses of facing stones survive and much of it exists only as a single course.

Denton Hall Turret

★★Visible remains★★: *turret (7b) and 65m section of Wall (Map 2). English Heritage. Free. On south side of the A186 (West Road; no parking). For access turn left (south) off West Road (A186) at the traffic lights by the Co-op into Broadwood Road and then take the first right (west) turn, called Turret Road. Head up here until the road curves sharply to the right and the Wall is visible in the grassy area ahead by the main road. A–Z Map p.40 B5. OS Ref. NZ 198655 (Sheet 88 1:50 000 Series).*

The first meaningful section of the Wall since Wallsend springs up at the bottom of the hill just across the Denton Burn about 1.2 miles (2km) to the west of Benwell. On the south side of West Road (A186) in a grassy enclosure, it includes turret 7b (**20**) containing a platform which probably formed a base either for a ladder or stairs to allow soldiers to reach upper floors and the Wall. It was recessed into the Wall and was therefore either put up at the same time as the Wall or earlier. The Wall itself here is entirely of 'Broad' dimensions, showing that this section was built to full width, and probably to full height, before the change to 'Narrow' dimensions.

20   *Denton Hall turret (7b) from the south-east. This is the first prominently visible section of Broad Wall. Built early in the Wall's development the turret and curtain are all of Broad Wall dimensions and do not show the off-sets visible further west.*

Substantial roadworks have taken place in recent years to create the Newcastle A1 by-pass. This runs north-south very shortly to the west beyond turret 7b, from which point the A186 becomes (as it once was in its entirety) the A69 Horsley-Heddon by-pass. As a by-product previously-invisible sections of Wall have been exposed on a berm to the south of the A69 immediately following the junction with the A1. To see them, leave the A69 150m west of the A1 interchange by turning left into the residential area and enter a road called, appropriately enough, The Ramparts, which runs parallel to the A69. This whole area has been heavily built-up in recent years and bears little resemblance to older maps.

Heddon-on-the-Wall

★★*Visible remains*★★: *stretch of Wall. English Heritage. Free. Parking on B6528 at Heddon. A–Z Map p. 36 A/B2. OS Ref. NZ 138668 (Sheet 88 1: 50 000 Series).*

The first long section of Wall lies further west at Heddon-on-the-Wall. To reach it carry along the A69 past the A1 interchange for about 0.7 mile (1.1km) until the next junction. Leave on the slip road and take the second left exit from the roundabout (B6528) to Heddon about 3.5 miles (6km) to the west.

At Heddon parking in a lay-by on the south side of the road is provided. The

21   The Wall at Heddon looking east. In the foreground is a medieval oven cut into the curtain. The Vallum is visible at upper centre right.

stretch of Broad Wall is impressive for length but not height – much of what remains is the lower course or two only. Unfortunately it also does not coincide with turrets or milecastles though a medieval kiln or oven can be seen, cut into the Wall (**21**). Milecastle 12 lay a few metres west of the visible section of Wall but later building has entirely destroyed its remains. Rebuilding of the curtain seems to have taken place here – a centurial stone of the year 158 found in the vicinity records that the VI Legion had 'rebuilt' something which must have been the Wall (Source 11).

To follow the Wall from Heddon drivers should head west on the B6318, and avoid the B6528 which now heads south-west to Hexham. The B6318 follows roughly the course of the Wall and the Military Road. About 1.3 miles (2km) further on is the site of the fort of Rudchester. Along the way sections of the Vallum are visible to the south of the road; the ditch is also visible from a point about 0.3 mile (0.5km) west of Heddon for a considerable distance.

RUDCHESTER FORT (*Vindobala*)

Nothing visible apart from traces of platform and ramparts. OS Ref. NZ 112675.

Built as a cavalry fort, Rudchester stands nearly 6.75 miles (11km) from

22   Altar from the mithraeum at Rudchester dedi-cated 'To the God' by Lucius Sentius Castus of the VI Legion. At the bottom Mithras is depicted wrestling with the sacred bull. Height 1.25m. (Photo: author, used with permission of Museum of Antiquities, Newcastle.)

Benwell and also projected north of the Wall. It has been partially excavated but apart from a gentle rise marking the 4.5 acre (1.8ha) fort platform nothing is visible at the site today and indeed is easily missed. In 1732 Horsley said that 'the ruins within the fort plainly appear' and were 'very remarkable'. The coming of the Military Road a few years later sounded the death-knell for the fort which was thereafter ransacked for stone.

The site lies immediately following a small crossroads. The meaning of the name is not clear but may mean something like 'white (or pleasant) high point'. The most interesting feature found so far was a mithraeum (now invisible) which lay a short distance to the south-west of the fort. It was first uncovered in 1844 but not excavated until 1953. The cult of Mithras, with its emphasis on virility, honour, valour, bravery, and male exclusivity, was popular amongst soldiers so it is no surprise that several are known from the vicinity of the Wall and other military sites in Britain.

The Rudchester mithraeum was a rickety-looking stone structure about 14m (46ft) in length which approximated to a crooked rectangle with an apse. Not surprisingly it suffered occasional collapse and rebuilding. One altar from here (now at Newcastle) shows that a centurion of the VI Legion, Lucius Sentius Castus, worshipped here (**22**). As the fort, like all those on the Wall, was manned by auxiliaries Castus probably served here as a member of a visiting detachment.

49

If urban development has put paid to most of the Wall in the Newcastle area then a combination of the Military Road and agriculture have seen off almost all the visible remnants from Benwell to Chesters. Sporadic appearances of the forward ditch and Vallum may reward the sharp-eyed but even the most assiduous Wall-walker or driver will have his or her work cut out to see much of consequence; even that will consist of little more than the occasional milecastle platform (14 and 15 can be spotted beside the road at NZ 106677 and NZ 092679 respectively). The Vallum can also be seen in the area of milecastle 18 running west from NZ 048684, and is very clear opposite a right (north) turn signposted to Moorhouse. It's always worth remembering though that much of the main road in this sector, following the eighteenth-century Military Road, lies right on top of the foundations of the Wall itself. Occasionally, despite the loss of the Wall, the Vallum and the ditch provide vivid reminders of the once-mighty Wall system.

DOWN HILL VALLUM
Vallum. OS Ref. NZ 008685

Just before the next fort at Haltonchesters is a remarkable sight. The Vallum is conspicuously visible on the approach to Down Hill, which the main road skirts to the north. Stop by the field gate to the west of the hill. Here a signpost marks a footpath to Haltonchesters to the south-west. Walk along a little way and look up at Down Hill. On the slope to the south the Vallum can be seen running over the hillside like a switchback and is in an excellent state of preservation.

HALTONCHESTERS FORT *Onnum*

Nothing visible apart from traces of platform and ramparts. OS Ref. NY 997685.

Like Rudchester, Haltonchesters holds no interest for a modern visitor. Even the topographer William Hutton 'passed through the centre of this Station without knowing it' nearly two centuries ago. The fort stands 7.2 miles (11.5km) west of Rudchester on a small plateau shortly after Down Hill. The 4.3 acre (1.7ha) site is marked by a small clump of trees and a large pair of stone gate posts to the south of the road which still runs on the Wall foundations here. The name *Onnum* is thought to derive from the Celtic word for water, probably thanks to the fact that a stream runs by the Wall here. It was built by soldiers from the VI Legion, who placed a commemorative inscription to Aulus Platorius Nepos on the west gate during the reign of Hadrian (Source 4). Further work was undertaken by the II Legion, probably during the reign of Antoninus Pius (**23**). Like Benwell and Rudchester, Haltonchesters protrudes north of the Wall and thus the modern road which runs on the Wall strikes

*23   Inscription from the fort at Haltonchesters dedicating work by the II Legion Augusta.
Undated but probably mid-second century. Width 0.84m. (Photo: author, used with permission of
Museum of Antiquities, Newcastle.)*

straight through the middle of the site.

The fort did have some unusual features. A bath-house, probably of late date, was built within the ramparts, and not outside as normal. It almost certainly replaced an earlier external bath-house; the same happened at Housesteads. The part of the fort to the south of the Wall was extended westwards around the end of the second century; and, a substantial fore-hall was put up opposite the headquarters building. The extension and this new building may have marked the installation of a first-rate cavalry unit which needed exercise and display areas (Source 4). However, the lack of apparent alternative access to the headquarters makes this interpretation a problem. Such halls are known to have existed in Britain thanks to an inscription at the outpost fort of Netherby, dating to 222, recording the final completion of a long-begun *basilica equester exercitatoria* ('cavalry exercise/training hall'). Unfortunately, the actual structure at Netherby has not been identified and never will be as it has long lain under a castle and a later house.

About 0.6 mile (1km) west of Haltonchesters the Roman north-south road now known as Dere Street crossed the Wall at Port Gate. John Horsley reported in 1732 that the remains of a Roman fortified gate still stood here, marking the crossing of the road. Probably laid out in the late first century during Agricola's campaigns, Dere Street came up from the south via Corbridge 2.5 miles (4km) away to the south and struck out north for the outpost forts at Risingham and High Rochester (see Chapter 7). This is a handy point to make a detour south to visit the major Roman base at Corbridge (see Chapter 8). In order to do so turn left onto the A68 and head south.

51

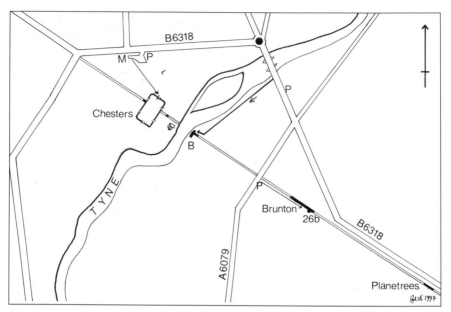

Map 3 *Planetrees to Chesters, approximately 1.25 miles (2km) east to west (not to scale).*
P = *Parking (follow direction of* ➤ *on foot). Planetrees section of Wall.* **26b** = *Turret 26b*
(Brunton). **B** = *Chesters Bridge abutment;* **M** = *Chesters Museum.*

Continuing on the Wall from Port Gate the ditch and Vallum start to become more frequently visible almost all of the 4.7 miles (7.4km) to Chesters. One find from this area is particularly unusual: a stone was recovered around 1 mile (1.6km) west of Haltonchesters marked FVLGVR DIV[OR]UM, meaning 'lightning of the gods' (now at Newcastle) and is thought to mark the spot where lightning struck perhaps either destroying a tree or injuring someone.

Milecastles 23 (NY 975689) and 24 (NY 961693) are both visible as low mounds to the south of the modern road but it is better to enjoy the Vallum. Here, in the vicinity of the Tyne, the fertile river valley has long made this area suitable for farming. Farmers need farmhouses and in locations close to Hadrian's Wall there were easy opportunities to acquire dressed stone.

PLANETREES

★★*Visible remains*★★: *15m section of Wall (Map 3). English Heritage (no sign on road). Free. Access south of the B6318 just west of Planetrees. OS Ref. NY 928696.*

At Planetrees, 1.1 miles (1.7km) east of Chesters, the Wall was undergoing systematic demolition in the early 1800s. The tragedy was recorded by William Hutton in 1801. A local farmer, called Henry Tulip, had taken the pragmatic decision to dismantle a 200m stretch which still stood more than 2.1m (7ft) high. Mr Tulip needed the masonry to build a farmhouse. At the time this was

24   *The Wall and turret at Brunton (26b) looking west towards Chesters fort.*

an entirely reasonable course of action and in those days there was no-one, or any law, to stop him doing what he wished with his own property. Hutton protested in vain at an argument he could 'regret, but not refute'.

A small section of the Wall survives near here on the long slope down to the west. Unfortunately, there is nowhere to park, and no English Heritage sign to mark the remains from the road. Nevertheless, there is a stile from the roadside and the Wall is in the field beyond. Look out for it on the left (south). The fragment shows well how the Broad foundation, and part of the curtain, had already been prepared here before the reduction of the Wall width. Just beyond the point of reduced width is a culvert under the Narrow Wall, let in to prevent water ponding and damaging the foundations.

Brunton Turret and Wall

Visible remains: *20m stretch of Wall and turret (26b) (Map 3). English Heritage. Free. Turn left at crossroads on the A6079. Park in lay-by on main road. OS Ref. NY 922698 (Sheet 87 1:50 000 Series).*

On the final approach to Chesters the road drops down into the valley of the North Tyne. The main road meets a crossroads with the A6079. Turn left (south) here and park a little way along in the lay-by on the left-hand side of the road in order to take a look at turret 26b (Brunton) and its associated stretch of Wall (**24**). This is the first well-preserved stretch of the curtain which

25   *The third-century eastern bridge abutment at Chesters. See also **26**.*

rises to a significant height. At least six courses of facing stones are visible, and the turret rises to 11 courses. The massive door step has visible grooves for the vertical slabs which formed the door jambs. There is a fine wing wall built to Broad Wall specifications on the east side of the turret. Inside is a weathered, and uninscribed, altar.

The Wall here points directly towards Chesters on the other side of the river to the west. Unfortunately, despite the stretch at Brunton, the Wall is no longer visible for the remaining distance to the river, apart from a small piece at the remains of the bridge over the Tyne.

Chesters Bridge abutment

★★Visible remains★★: Roman bridge abutment (Map 3). English Heritage. Free. Difficult parking on A6079 just before the single-carriageway modern bridge. OS Ref. NY 915701 (Sheet 87 1:50 000 Series).

Head back up the A6079 from Brunton turret and turn left (north-west), following signs to Chollerford, to continue on the B6318 for a very short distance down the hill. The road narrows as it approaches the modern road bridge across the Tyne. Park off the north side of the road opposite Chollerford Garage, and walk down to the footpath to the Roman bridge which is just before the traffic lights here on the south side of the road. The step leads down to the cinder path leading the half mile (0.8km) to the bridge abutment which

26   *Detail of the third-century bridge abutment at Chesters showing the incorporated Hadrianic bridge pier. Note the cut-outs for clamps.*

is one of the most important sites on the Wall system (**25**).

Here Hadrian's Wall became a substantial bridge over the Tyne. Today just a short stretch of Wall is visible running up to a monumental bridge abutment. This lies high and dry because the river has moved slightly westwards since antiquity. Conversely, the corresponding abutment on the opposite bank is now submerged (though part of the guardhouse has been exposed in the opposite riverbank). The visible east abutment is of third-century date and was probably constructed during the Severan programme of rebuilding and repairs on the Wall. It consisted of an enormous masonry pier capped with a tower within which was a mill. The water-race for the mill can still be seen. All around are scattered the remains of blocks uncovered during excavations. The small rectangular hole in the stones is called a 'lewis-hole' which is wider inside than its opening suggests. It was used for lifting by means of a rope with a metal device attached to the end. The metal device was inserted into the hole and expanded under load; the shape of the whole prevented it coming out and thus the stone could be lifted into position. One of the blocks facing outwards from the abutment on the north side has a phallus carved on its face. The phallus was a totemic Roman device used to ward off the 'evil eye' and serve as a good-luck charm. It was also commonly placed over entrances to houses, and any other point of transit from one environment to another.

Under Hadrian the bridge was a smaller-scale affair carried on eight modest stone piers. One of these can be spotted by tracing the outline of the blocks immediately to the west of the tower's lower courses (**26**). In the early third century this was replaced by a vastly more substantial stone bridge with three huge piers. The new bridge seems to have had various decorative features such as an arch and a pair of columns at either end. There may have been a practical reason for the rebuilding: the old bridge might have been damaged or even destroyed by floods. Both bridges were evidently wide enough for wheeled traffic and as they are continuations of the Wall it has been suggested that they are evidence for the Wall having had a walkway on its top. But this does not necessarily follow and cannot be proved.

To reach Chesters fort, tantalisingly close across the river (the bath-house is easily visible from the bridge abutment), return to the main road and cross the Tyne by the modern bridge. Turn immediately left (west) at the roundabout over the bridge and follow the B6318 for 0.3 mile (0.5km) to the car-park at Chesters.

3. Chesters to Housesteads

CHESTERS (*Cilurnum*)

★★Visible remains★★: fort and bath-house (Map 3). English Heritage. Entrance fee. Open all year round (9.30–6.00 1 April–30 September; 10.00–5.00 1–31 October, 10.00–4.00 in winter). Tel: 01434–681379. Head west on the B6318 from Chollerford just beyond the Tyne crossing, and turn left at the signpost to Chesters shortly afterwards. OS Ref. NY 912705 for the entrance (Sheet 87 1:50 000 Series).

Entering the grounds in which Chesters lies looks like turning into the gardens of a substantial private country house. And that is precisely what it is. The site was purchased in 1796 by Nathaniel Clayton. His son, John Clayton the antiquary, excavated the buildings visible here and made his home a shrine to the Wall. The museum collection here is largely made up of his finds from Chesters and other Wall sites. In many respects the location is the most unrepresentative of all the Wall forts for it lies in the fertile and sheltered valley of the Tyne surrounded by substantial trees and overlooked by Clayton's house. The name *Cilurnum* may mean 'large pool', and probably referred to the proximity of the river.

The 5.8 acre (2.3ha) fort is relatively well-preserved, thanks to Clayton's ownership of the site, and the accumulation of soil over the remains. A number of internal buildings have been exposed but, apart from the gateways, the ramparts are still buried. Each building is fenced off from the surrounding meadow with the result that, despite having some of the most conspicuous internal remains on the Wall apart from those at Housesteads, the fort is difficult to envisage as a whole.

Access is through the ticket office. Immediately ahead and to the right is the Clayton Memorial Museum. Leave that for the moment and bear left down a path which heads towards the north gate of the fort (**27**). Water, taken from somewhere to the north, was channelled into a tank in the eastern guardroom of this gate between 177–84 (Source 16). At a later date a covered conduit was built through the eastern entrance of the gate.

Inside the fort two barrack blocks are visible to the left. They aren't

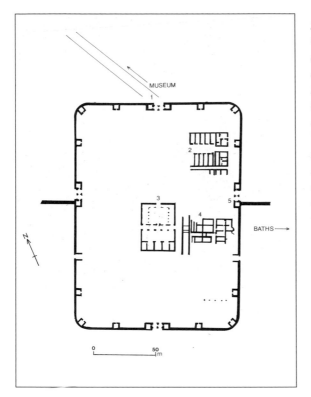

*27   Plan of the fort at Chesters. Of the ramparts only the gates and towers are exposed. **1** North gate. **2** Barracks. **3** Headquarters building. **4** Commanding officer's house. **5** East gate and Wall. Prior to the fort's construction the Wall crossed the site with turret 27a located between the Headquarters building and the Commanding officer's house.*

completely exposed but show the rows of rooms, each of which was home to ten men, and a large room at the end which accommodated their centurion. Straight ahead is the headquarters building. To the north was an open courtyard surrounded on three sides by a covered portico. On the fourth (south) side was the cross-hall. At the back of the hall were the various rooms for regimental valuables and standards. One of the rooms, the *aedes*, incorporated a subterranean chamber which, when discovered in the late eighteenth century by local 'rustics' (so described by Collingwood Bruce), still had the remains of its oak door. This disintegrated almost immediately on exposure to fresh air (**28**).

One of the headquarters-building strongroom steps turned out to be a reused, but undated, stone (now in the museum) bearing the name of the First Cohort of Dalmatians, an infantry unit which probably formed part of the Chesters garrison at some point in the late second century. Chesters was a cavalry fort and in the late second and third century it was certainly also garrisoned by the Second Ala of Asturians. However, the documents from Vindolanda have shown that the presence of two or more different units at the same fort was not unusual.

Prior to the fort's construction the Wall passed across the site on the line of the headquarters building's north wall. It was demolished along with turret 27a which lay just outside the headquarters building's north-east corner.

28   *The entrance and stairs to the subterranean strongroom in the Chesters fort headquarters building.*

Immediately beside the headquarters building to the east is the commanding officer's personal house. It had its own bath-suite and hypocaust, parts of which can be seen beside the tree still growing amongst the remains.

All six fort gates are exposed. The most interesting is the east gate which retains the springer for one of its arches. The worn recesses for the door pivots can be seen in some cases along with the iron collar which was designed to limit wear to the slabs.

Chesters projected north of the Wall, so this gate and the twin-portalled east and west gates are on the north side of the curtain. Short sections of the Wall can be seen attached to the south guard-rooms on the east and west gates. Like most similar forts Chesters had additional single-portalled east and west gates south of the Wall. A diploma of the year 146 supplying the name of the governor, Papirius Aelianus (Source 25), was found in the south gate and is now in the British Museum, but a replica is on display here at Chesters.

Bath-house

None of the fort buildings is as impressive now as the bath-house which lies to the east on the steep slope down to the river. Visitors to the bridge abutment on the far bank (see p. 54) cannot fail to have noticed it. Soil and rubble from the slope filled up the building early in its dereliction thereby preventing further disintegration and concealing it from anyone looking for a handy supply of stone. As a result some of its walls still stand to 3m (10ft) in height.

The bath-house (**29**) is entered by the Roman door in the north wall. This is the *apodyterium* or changing room; the niches in the west wall were perhaps

29   *Chesters bath-house from the south.*

the equivalent of lockers or they may have contained honorific mementos. The rest of the building is very complicated, with the various rooms being altered in form and function throughout the structure's history. In fact it was not even recognized as a bath-house when it was discovered in the late nineteenth century; Collingwood Bruce suggested in 1885 that perhaps it had been 'intended to defend the passage of the river' before it its 'final destruction' by fire. But once clearance had been finished in 1886 the building's true identity was recognized.

Leave the changing room by the door in the south wall and enter a small chamber. The door in the opposite wall leads to a long rectangular room which was once a dry-heat room, or *laconicum*, and later a warm room, *tepidarium*, with beyond the hot room, *caldarium*. More hot rooms lay parallel to these on the east. The door to the right leads to the new *laconicum* which replaced the old one. The door to the left leads to the cold room, *frigidarium* (**30**).

More interesting than the minor detail of the rooms was the bath-house's roofing. Hot, wet air is a sure way to rot roof timbers, quite apart from the fire risk of using wood in a building heated by a furnace. Bath-houses thus needed more durable roofs. At Chesters a lightweight vault was created by using blocks of tufa to make curved ribs. Cutouts in the tufa blocks created brackets to support thin pieces of tile to fill the gaps. In this way nearly half the volume of the roof was void. Even so, vaults create lateral thrusts, and these have the effect of pushing side walls outwards. Being built on a slope the side of the bath-house closest to the river was already under some stress. In order to counter these effects the east wall of the bath-house was reinforced with

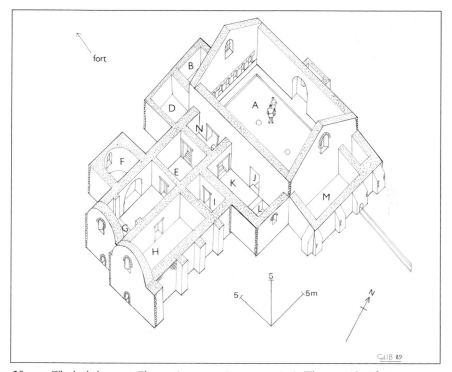

30 *The bath-house at Chesters (axonometric reconstruction). The room identifications were made by G. MacDonald in 1931. **A** Apodyterium (changing room) - note the niches, perhaps for storing clothes. **N** Vestibule. **K** Frigidarium (cold room). **L** Early cold bath. **J** Later cold bath. **E** Laconicum (dry-heat room). **I** Tepidarium (moist warm room). **H** Second tepidarium, with buttresses to support the building against the downward slope to the river. **F** and **G** Caldaria (moist hot rooms). Room **G** contained a number of tufa and tile components which have been identified as parts of a vaulted roof. Ribs of tufa were connected with two rows of flat tiles to create cavities between each rib, thus saving weight. **M** Latrine. Furnaces were sited by **B**'s north wall, and by **G**'s, and **H**'s south walls.*

substantial buttresses, the lower courses of which are still clearly visible.

By the riverbank near the bath-house, work is in progress to limit erosion. As a result, part of the guardhouse which formed part of the bridge abutment on this side of the river has been exposed. More may come to light in the near future.

Museum

Just outside the entrance is a large misshapen boulder bearing the carved words *Petra Flavi Carantini*, 'the rock of Flavius Carantinus'. It came from the nearby quarry at Fallowfield Fell where Flavius Carantinus carved his name in the rock face at some unspecified time during the Wall's construction or later repairs. It's one of many such examples, but most are still *in situ* or weathered

31 *Statue from Chesters of a goddess on a heifer; identification uncertain but may be Julia Mammaea, mother of the emperor Severus Alexander (221–35) as Juno, or as the eastern mother goddess Cybele. Julia was killed along with her son in the year 235. Height 1.6 m.*

away. Inside, look out for the statue of a goddess or empress on a cow (**31**), the carved phallus (**32**), and the centurial stones (**4**) which were placed in the Wall by the military or civilian unit responsible for a particular stretch. Many of the most important inscriptions from the Wall are stored here (such as Source 5).

Some of the items recovered from the water shrine to Coventina at Carrawburgh (p. 66; **36**) can be seen in the museum, including altars and the two curious pottery vessels in a red fabric. Looking not unlike a pair of crude, but ornate Victorian chimney pots, these were probably incense burners. They were the handiwork of one Saturninus Gabinius who inscribed his name and dedication to Coventina on them. Another unique find in the museum is the corn measure(?) from the fort at Carvoran (**53**). Made of bronze and looking like an upturned bucket this apparently predates the Wall for it bears the defaced name and titles of Domitian (81-96). Its height is 31cm (12.2in) and it contained 17.5 Roman *sextarii* according to the inscription (a little over two modern gallons). It actually takes more than the stated capacity, thought by some to indicate that the Roman authorities were cheating locals when requisitions or taxes were paid in kind. However, this overlooks the stupidity of stating the capacity of any vessel to be its maximum. Any normal measuring container has an upper mark below the top.

32 *Block from Chesters carved with a phallus. The phallus was a familiar Roman symbol which represented not just fertility but also good luck, and served also as a defence against the 'evil eye'. It was a popular motif for placing over points of entry such as doors or gates. Width 300mm.*

Blackcarts Turret

★★*Visible remains*★★: *turret (29a) and 200m length of Wall 1.75 miles (3km) west of Chesters (Map 4). Park on right turn (north) from B6318 just past the remains up a narrow minor road and park by the hedge. English Heritage. Free. OS Ref. NY 885713 (Sheet 87 1:50 000 Series).*

Heading west from Chesters the B6318 returns to the line of the Wall and starts to climb to the central, and most barren, section of the Wall system. It is correspondingly better-preserved because the Wall here has suffered significantly less from the effects of agriculture and removal of stone. Stretches of Vallum and ditch are clearly visible on either side of the road. The site of milecastle 29 at Tower Tye may be seen (NY 889711). Shortly afterwards the road makes a slight left turn and loses height before rising up again. By the road here a long stretch of Wall is visible to the north, and includes turret 29a (**33**). The turret, which was excavated in 1873 and 1971, lies some way back down the slope. Unlike the example at Brunton this turret was built for the Broad Wall, a fact made by plain by the wing walls on either side. Its outer walls are mostly reduced to their lowest courses; it may have been demolished during the Roman period but coin finds suggest it might have stayed in use up to the fourth century. This is unusual for any Wall turret, most of which are believed to have been demolished from the late second century on (though this is very uncertain and the process may have taken place over centuries rather than decades). Just to the north the ditch can be clearly seen.

33   Blackcarts turret (29a), Wall and ditch looking east. The turret is visible in the middle distance.

LIMESTONE CORNER

★★*Visible remains*★★: *unfinished ditch 2.5 miles (4km) west of Chesters (Map 4). Park by field-gate on north side of B6318. OS Ref. NY 875715 (Sheet 87 1:50 000 Series).*

One of the most striking features of the whole Wall system can be seen at Limestone Corner a little over 0.7 mile (1.1km) further on. Just beyond the hill the Vallum can be seen to the south in remarkable detail a few metres from the road (**34**). Note the crossings inserted across its ditch. What makes this section unusual is the large number of huge blocks abandoned by the Roman military engineers. To the north of the road (and the Wall) the builders gave up any attempt to complete the forward ditch, so clearly visible a little way back at Blackcarts. The rock was broken up by chiselling holes into it and inserting wedges. The wedges were soaked with water, which then expanded and split the rock. Here, however, the rock here simply proved too resilient, and to this day the ditch is filled with enormous blocks (**35**). One slab still defiantly in place retains visible wedge holes. However, the Vallum was completed here to the south of the Wall, in spite of the problems, and shows it was an absolute priority.

34   The Vallum at Limestone Corner looking west; note the large number of scattered blocks extracted from the cutting by the builders. The road (B6318) at upper right runs along the line of the Wall.

Parking at Limestone Corner is difficult and potentially extremely dangerous. Great care is needed by those heading west to make a successful manoeuvre across the road to park by the field-gate on the north side. If the opportunity is missed then it's much safer to carry on and turn round. Heading back east the blocks in the ditch are easily seen to the north (now left) of the road with a small hard-standing by the field-gate about 100m west of the blocks.

Now leave Limestone Corner and head west on the B6318 for the fort at Carrawburgh 1 mile (1.6km) beyond. The landscape is noticeably wilder and bleaker. The road is narrower and care should be taken on sharp dips and rises. There is little opportunity either for overtaking or turning.

CARRAWBURGH (*Brocolitia*)

★★*Visible remains*★★: *fort platform (privately-owned) and Temple of Mithras (Map 4). English Heritage. Free. Parking on south side of B6318 east of the fort platform. OS Ref. NY 859712 (Sheet 88 1:50 000 Series).*

Leaving Limestone Corner the road passes the site of milecastle 31 a few metres before reaching the visitors' car-park for the fort of Carrawburgh. Its ancient name of *Brocolitia* ('heathery spot' or 'rocky spot') is more appropriate

35   *The ditch at Limestone Corner looking north-east. The ditch and berm are covered with abandoned boulders and blocks.*

to its appearance nowadays. The site commands an excellent view to the south across the valley created by the stream which runs south from a point west of the fort, once the site of Coventina's Well.

Carrawburgh was not part of the first arrangement of forts on the Wall. In most cases the diversion of the Vallum around them shows that their sites were planned, even if not yet built on. But the Vallum runs under the 3.9-acre (1.6ha) fort here. It had to be filled in before the latter was built. The site has been barely touched by excavation but is thought to have been built around the year 130 (Source 6), though the evidence is far from conclusive. Various units are testified on inscriptions from the site but many may only represent individuals who had come to pay their respects at Carrawburgh's remarkable shrines. Visitors may walk over the fort platform, which is still in private hands, but apart from hollows marking the sites of the west gate and an interval tower (containing part of a huge carved block) in the west rampart there is nothing to see.

Coventina's Well

At Carrawburgh only the Mithraeum is visible today but the nearby shrine of Coventina was once the scene of a remarkable discovery. The 'well' lay west of the fort at the point where a spring rises a few metres south of the modern road. The spring, and a Roman enclosure wall, were noted by Horsley in 1732. But, according to Bruce, the spring had dried up by the middle of the nineteenth century thanks to a nearby leadmine draining off supplies, and its

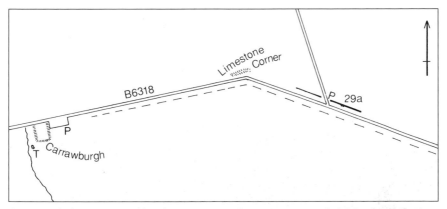

Map 4 *Blackcarts to Carrawburgh via Limestone Corner, approximately 2.25 miles (3.5km) east to west (not to scale).* **P** *= Parking.* **29a** *= Turret 29a (Blackcarts).* **T** *= Temple of Mithras. The dotted line indicates the Vallum.*

location lost. However, the leadminers unwittingly found the spring in 1876 when, as he recorded, they started hunting for a lead vein:

Coming in contact with the upper courses of the stone framework of the well, they rightly thought that further search in that spot was vain, and went elsewhere. Mr Clayton, hearing that the well described by Horsley and others had been hit upon, thought it desirable that it should at once be properly explored, and gave directions accordingly. Covering the mouth of the well were some large stones, which had probably been taken from the upper courses of its containing walls and thrown, for the purpose of concealment, upon the mass of treasure of which the well had been made the recipient. On the removal of these stones ... a mass of coins, chiefly of the lower empire [i.e. of third- and fourth-century date], met the gaze of the excavators. Then carved stones, altars, coins, vases, Roman pearls, old shoes, fibulae [brooches], and other Roman remains were met with in an indiscriminate mass...

Clayton and Bruce assumed that this was a panic dumping of treasure from the fort in the face of some barbarian onslaught. This was a typical, but attractive, antiquarian interpretation. Despite appreciating that the well was likely to be a sacred spot dedicated to the goddess Coventina, who was named on several stones and other artefacts, they did not recognize that the contents had accumulated over a very long time. The spring had once been surrounded by a wall, perhaps the footings of a cover building. Here, in a small pool innumerable gifts, including at least 22 altars and two pottery incense burners (now in Chesters Museum), had been deposited as gifts to Coventina or other deities (**36**). Perhaps the most remarkable find was the enormous quantity of coins – at least 13,487 were found but many were swiftly acquired by unofficial visitors at the time. The true figure may have exceeded 16,000. Many of the coins were extremely worn and John Collingwood Bruce arranged for them to be melted down in December 1879 and cast into an eagle weighing 6.5 kg.

67

36   Relief from Coventina's Well at Carrawburgh dedicated to the goddess by the commander, Titus D[omitius?] Cosconianus, of the First Cohort of Batavians, stationed at the fort. Early third century. Height 0.74m.

Nothing of the shrine can be seen now apart from the spring, though even this is just a marshy hollow of no interest.

Mithraeum

Nearby stands the Mithraeum which is one of several known along the Wall but the only one visible today. It stands on the east bank of the valley of the stream just below the south-west corner of the fort. Access today is via the metalled track from the car-park. It runs alongside the east rampart of the fort diverting south-west to lead directly to the Mithraeum enclosure.

The Mithraeum was discovered in 1949 after a period of drought allowed some of the stonework to protrude above ground. It is usually quite evident here that the location has drainage problems and the temple is often rather wet and muddy (**37**). Mithras was an eastern warrior god of Persian, not Roman, origins, and was associated with strength and the power of good over evil. This was manifested in the myth that, in a cave, Mithras slaughtered a bull who had been created at the dawning of time. In this way he released vital life forces which had been contained in the bull's blood.

Exclusive to men, the cult's emphasis on honour and valour appealed to soldiers. Mithraea are thus not uncommon on military sites. Like early churches mithraea were small versions of the Roman basilica with its nave and aisles, normally used for civic government buildings or military halls. The

*37   Interior of the Carrawburgh Mithraeum looking north down the centre of the nave
towards the altars (the originals are in Newcastle). The short vertical posts are casts of the remains
of full-height timbers which supported the roof.*

form of building was suited to congregations, so it is not at all surprising that
it was used in a number of applications. But mithraea were sunk into the
ground and had no windows. Darkness and artificial light were used to
heighten a sense of mystic gloom in an effort to emulate the cave in which
Mithras had killed the bull. The modern state of the Carrawburgh Mithraeum
could thus hardly be less representative of its original form.

Within, the lower parts of statues of Mithras' two associates Cautes and
Cautopates are visible. These, like the altars at the far end, are modern
reproductions (the originals are at Newcastle, where a reconstruction of the
temple's interior has been built). There was also a statue of a goddess within
the door but repeated theft of replicas has meant this is no longer represented.
Originally the aisles had raised floors, revetted by wattle which is represented
today with concrete casts. The rectangular concrete blocks mark the square
timber posts which supported the roof. At the far end three altars faced the
dedicants. One incorporated slits so that a theatrical effect might be created
with a lamp behind the altar. Two name prefects of the First Cohort of
Batavians, in garrison here in the early third century (Source 18). In the apse
above a stone reredos, depicting the slaying of the bull, would have been set
into the wall.

This Mithraeum began life as a simple rectangle. It was later extended and a
square apse added. An 'ordeal' pit was dug into the floor perhaps so that the

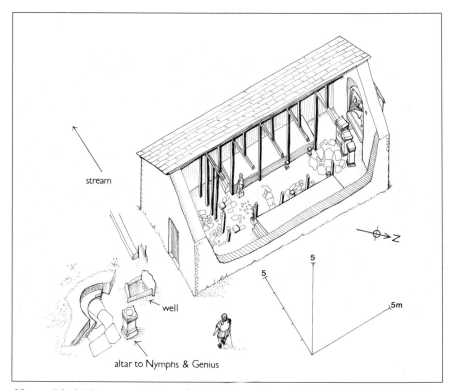

stream

well

altar to Nymphs & Genius

38   *The Mithraeum and Shrine of the Nymphs at Carrawburgh. This drawing shows the temple as it may have appeared in the fourth century. Note the altars within and the reredos sculpture of the sacred act of killing the bull. The Shrine of the Nymphs lay immediately outside the entrance.*

faithful could undergo initiation ceremonies involving burial, though it may have had other functions. In the fourth century the apse was compressed and some of the statues were moved about while the ordeal pit was filled in. Subsequently it seems to have been destroyed rather than allowed to fall into ruin. The reredos was smashed to pieces and the building abandoned.

Immediately outside the entrance to the Mithraeum, but invisible today apart from a slab protruding from the ground, was a little outdoor nymphaeum (**38**). Consisting of no more than a well, a semi-circular stone seat, and a hard-standing with an altar it was dedicated to the *genius*, or spirit of the place and nymphs. The presence of this little shrine, Coventina's Well, and the Mithraeum suggest that perhaps Carrawburgh was an important Wall religious area. It was quite normal in the Roman world for a multitude of cults to be represented at a single place of special significance. The Younger Pliny described just such a gathering of shrines at the source of the 'Clitumnus' in Umbria in Italy (*Letters* viii.8). Although the Mithraeum was an unequivocally Roman-period structure the other two shrines may well have had pre-Roman origins.

39   *Coesike turret (33b) from the south-east looking west towards Sewingshields Crags.*

The Mithraeum was just one of a large number of buildings in the fort's hinterland, now marked by pits and scattered blocks. They formed its external settlement. Little or nothing is known about this small village apart from the presence of a bath-house between Coventina's Well and the Mithraeum. The whole site has yet to fulfil its potential.

West from Carrawburgh the road once more runs along the line of the Wall. The site of milecastle 32 lies to the south of the road at NY 845710, but shortly afterwards the road moves south of the Wall; milecastle 33 appears as a mound to the north of the road at NY 831707 1.75 miles (3km) from the fort. A little under 0.6 mile (1km) from milecastle 33 the modern road makes a sharp left turn into a hollow, cutting across the Vallum which comes sweeping up from the south, reappearing on the north side. It's a magnificent sight.

SEWINGSHIELDS CRAGS TURRETS AND MILECASTLES

★★Visible remains★★: *turrets 33b and 34a, milecastle 35, and turret 35a. English Heritage. Free. OS Ref. NY 822705 (Coesike turret, 33b) and 805702 (Sewingshields milecastle, 35) (Sheet 87 1:50 000 Series).*

From hereon the Wall system moves north of the modern road and access is either by foot or from side roads. To see turret 33b (**39**) at Coesike take the public footpath labelled Sewingshields, on the north side of the B6318, from just before the corner described in the preceding paragraph. Parking is

71

impossible and forward planning is necessary to drop walkers or to walk here from a distance. The turret, with its Broad Wall wings, lies approximately 200m west from the corner, and a little over 100m north of the modern road. It was demolished in the late second century and its door, and recess into the Wall blocked up.

Hadrian's Wall now makes for the higher ground, taking advantage of the north-facing crags. They made the ditch redundant and it peters out near the site of milecastle 34 0.3 mile (0.5km) beyond Coesike turret. The Vallum diverts to travel further south in the lower-lying land where it was not only easier to raise mounds and dig ditches, but was also probably the only place where it was possible. Walkers may like to continue on foot from here to Housesteads, but the 3 miles (4.5km) can be quite challenging, especially across Sewingshields Crags. The appeal is more aesthetic than instructive as not much of the Wall is visible until the final approaches to Housesteads just as the Wall crosses the Knag Burn. What can be seen is Narrow Wall on Broad Wall foundations, but at only about 2m in width it may well be attributable to third-century rebuilding under Septimius Severus.

Turret 34a is visible at NY 813704. Unlike Coesike turret its Broad Wall wings are unusually short but it shared the same fate of being demolished and its recess filled in, though part of this filling has now been removed. Turret 34b lies under a farmhouse. Milecastle 35 (Sewingshields), at NY 805702, is a tumbledown affair which seems to have ended its life in the Roman period as a metal-working centre. The milecastle lacks a north gate but it isn't certain whether this feature was omitted when it was first built. The steep drop would certainly have made it unnecessary but at milecastle 37 (**46**) a north gate was included under not dissimilar conditions. At Sewingshields the gate may have been removed and the milecastle's north wall entirely reconstructed at a later date.

The Wall hugs the crags and shortly afterwards reaches the site of turret 35a, demolished like 33b and 34a. Beyond it makes a sharp turn to head almost due south for about half a mile (0.8km). The ditch makes a brief reappearance at King's Wicket (NY 798695) before the Wall climbs to the site of milecastle 36 on King's Hill. From here Housesteads fort is about 0.6 mile (1km) to the south-west.

4. Housesteads to Cawfields

HOUSESTEADS (*Vercovicium*)

Visible remains: *fort, Wall and walk to milecastle 37 (see below) (Map 5). English Heritage. Entrance fee (free to National Trust members). Open all year round. (9.30–6.00 1 April–30 September; 10.00–5.00 1–31 October, 10.00–4.00 in winter). Tel: 01434–344363. Access from the B6318 into car-park beside main road. Access to the fort is by foot up a steep path and is difficult for disabled visitors. OS Ref. NY 790687 (fort), 794684 car-park (Sheet 87 1:50 000 Series; Sheet 546 1:25 000 Series).*

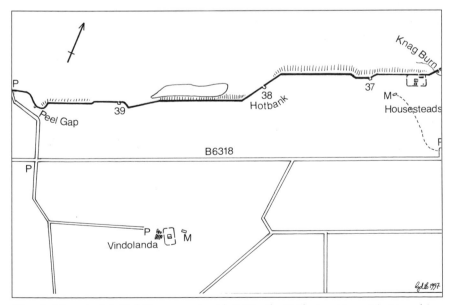

Map 5 *Housesteads to Peel Gap, approximately 2.75 miles (4.5km) east to west (not to scale).*
P = *Parking.* **M** = *Museum.* **37, 38,** *and* **39** = *Milecastles.*

40   *Housesteads fort from the car-park. The Wall passes from right to left beyond the ridge. The terracing of the internal buildings to accommodate the slope can be appreciated in this view.*

Housesteads (*Vercovicium*, the 'place of able fighters') is reached on foot from the car-park on the B6318 some 5 miles (8.5km) west from Carrawburgh. The fort is the busiest on the whole Wall because there is more to be seen here than anywhere else. During summer the car-park can be extremely congested. The Visitors Centre beside the car-park is managed by the National Trust but the fort itself is now in the care of English Heritage.

From the car-park the 5-acre (2ha) fort can be seen slapped across the ridge like a wet flannel, emphasizing its commanding position (**40**). All the ramparts are exposed, as are a number of the internal buildings, and unlike Chesters it is still visibly integrated with the Wall (**41**). It was an infantry fort, garrisoned probably in the third century by the nominally 1000-strong First Cohort of Tungrians (the same unit so well-known from the writing tablets of a century earlier at Vindolanda). The many inscriptions which record their presence here cannot be precisely dated.

The steep walk up to the fort can take 10–15 minutes. On the way terraces can be seen below the fort; these are the remains of cultivation terraces, used by the fort and *vicus* inhabitants taking advantage of the south-facing slope. In 1801 Hutton was able to count 'twenty streets' in what he described as a 'very large Suburb'. Some of the *vicus* buildings are exposed south of the fort but uneven ridges in the ground show that structures lie buried right round the south of the fort and outside its west rampart. Such *vici* lay outside almost every long-term fort in the Roman Empire. Here, the settlement seems to have been obliged to develop south of the Vallum, and thus outside the military zone, but

74

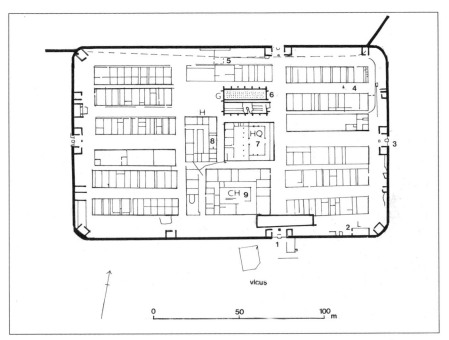

41   *Plan of the fort at Housesteads. 1 South gate. 2 Latrine. 3 East gate. 4 Barracks.*
5 pre-fort alignment of the Wall and turret 36b. 6 Granaries. 7 Headquarters building.
8 Hospital(?). 9 Commanding officer's house.

was later allowed to encroach the fort. One of the buildings, when excavated, was found to contain an adult couple buried under the floor; not unreasonably this was interpreted as evidence of murder. A mithraeum lay in the western part of the valley below the fort, but nothing is visible today.

The path leads past the south wall of the fort to the ticket office; visitors who enter the fort without a ticket will be directed to the ticket office where there is also a small museum and shop. Walkers from Coesike turret and Sewingshields will arrive at Housesteads by the east gate. They should pass round the south wall of the fort and obtain tickets before returning to the south gate.

The latrine and south defences

The best place to enter is through the south gate. It was adapted into a fortified farmhouse, known as a 'bastle house', in the Middle Ages when Housesteads was the headquarters of a family of border cattle-thieves. Most of these additions have been removed. Turn right within and walk along the inside of the south wall towards the south-east corner, passing the remains of stone steps which provided access to the rampart. Just beyond is the latrine (**42**). The wooden squat seats have long since vanished but were arranged in rows around three of the walls. Water was fed in from the adjacent cistern down a gravity-powered conduit. It then ran around a channel at foot level so that feet and

42   *Housesteads latrine in the south-east corner of the fort from the north-west. At upper left and lower right are the remains of water tanks. In the centre right steps which must once have led up to the rampart can be seen.*

posteriors could be washed with clean water. The dirty water ran off into a deep passage beneath the seats, flushing out excrement through a channel in the fort wall.

Beyond the latrine is the south-east angle interval tower. The ramparts of all the forts were reinforced with simple towers at the corners and in the long stretches between corners and gates. These were simple structures, tacked on to the walls. An entrance at the bottom provided access either to a stair or ladder to the higher levels. There were probably doorways on the first floor to allow access to the rampart walkway. Examples illustrated on Trajan's Column show these either with pitched or flat roofs and always seem to have had upper chambers with windows looking out.

The east gate

Follow the fort wall round to the east gate, noting here the pivot holes for the gates, and the wheel ruts. On the roadway a fragmentary carving of a Victory in a niche (now at Chesters) was found in 1852. It probably came from the superstructure of the east gate (**43**), perhaps facing out over the road above one of the arches and flanking a dedicatory inscription, with Mars on the other side. In time the gate seems to have become semi-derelict. When the south guardchamber was cleared a large amount of coal was found inside, suggesting it had become a coalshed in late Roman times. The south entrance had been thoroughly blocked up, apparently utilising some components of the gate's

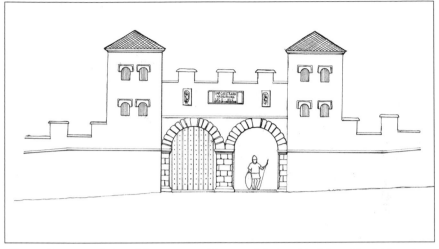

43   *Reconstructed view of the east gate at Housesteads in its original form. The height and form of the towers and crossing above the portals are hypothetical.*

superstructure which had either collapsed or been dismantled. A vertical channel was cut into the outside of the central pier, perhaps to accommodate a timber upright for some kind of botched gate arrangement made out of what was left of the old one and what could be knocked up out of planks and blocks. It's difficult to imagine what this must have looked like other than a kind of tumbledown last-stand encampment. But after two centuries or more of weathering, structural decay and perhaps indifference, the only alternative would have been to demolish it and start again. Evidently the wherewithal, discipline, and motivation to do that were lacking.

Knag Burn gateway

Leave the fort by the east gate and follow the fort wall up to where it engaged with the Wall proper. It's worth taking a look at some of the external ramparts of the fort and noticing the different-sized blocks at some places on higher levels. These represent on-going Roman repairs to the walls, and are especially clear on the south side. Many of the larger blocks are thought to have come from the fort gates in the late Roman period when they had become semi-ruinous. To the east of Housesteads the Wall crossed the Knag Burn and a channel was provided under the Wall to let the stream pass. The fort bath-house was built to the south along the stream's valley but was heavily robbed out in the eighteenth century.

The Knag Burn was the site of a gateway through the Wall. There were very few transit points through the Wall other than those at forts and milecastles. However, it is self-evident at Housesteads that trans-Wall traffic would have to climb the very steep road up to the north gate to enter the fort. There was such a road but it apparently fell out of use quite early on. It was far simpler to let a gate in through the convenient little valley, though evidence from the structure suggests it was not constructed until the fourth century. The gate had two sets of doors, creating a kind of 'airlock'; it has been presumed that this allowed traffic to be contained for examination, and perhaps the exaction of duties without leaving gates dangerously open and exposed to attack. In this respect it was a little like a miniature milecastle.

The barracks

Now re-enter the fort by the east gate. Ahead is a structure which began life as a storehouse and seems to have been altered into a late bath-house, perhaps replacing the external bath-house by the Knag Burn. To the right (north-west), are the stone footings of parallel barrack blocks. They may very well have had timber superstructures. In the Hadrianic period these were built as single structures with contiguous internal chambers. Each would have provided accommodation for a 'century', a unit of 80 men. In the fourth century these were replaced with rows of individual chambers.

Pass along to the north gate. Although twin-portalled like all the others the steep approach up to the fort here not only led to the ramp to the north gate being abandoned, but it seems that the eastern half of the gate was never even used. It was eventually taken apart, piece by piece, and the slabs used for blocking up the entrance. The western entrance was used for long enough to become worn but by the late-Roman period it was no more than a single-portalled foot gate. The gate is reasonably well-preserved. The internal central pier stands five courses high and a water tank stands inside the fort beside the western gate-tower.

Turret 36b

About 30m west of the north gate and a few metres south of a point roughly in the middle of the fort's north wall are the remains of turret 36b which, with the Wall, was built here to Broad Wall specifications in the early stages of the Wall's construction. Wall and turret were cleared away when the fort was built, its north wall being constructed a few metres north of the turret. The turret's foundations have now been exposed and can be seen between buildings clinging to the fort's north wall and a barrack block to the south. As might be expected, they are at a noticeably lower level.

This is an excellent place to see how the fort was built across the steep slope. A few metres to the south-east lie two substantial stone granaries, with their solid buttresses. The buttresses resisted the lateral thrust created by settling grain and also helped support the roofing. The southern granary still has the visible remains of a medieval oven built into it.

Headquarters building

Beyond the granaries to the south is the headquarters building and to the right (west) the hospital. This followed standard military pattern, facing east with an entrance probably decorated with reliefs of Mars and Victory (**44**). Within was a forecourt with covered porticoes on three sides and the cross-hall on the

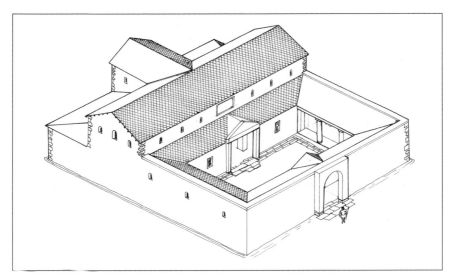

44   *Reconstructed isometric view of the Housesteads headquarters building in its Hadrianic form looking north-west. The rooms to the rear seem to have had upper storeys added to them at a later date.*

fourth (**45**). The figure of Mars survives (at Chesters), and the Victory may have been the one standing on a globe now at Newcastle (it had been removed to outside the fort by the early eighteenth century). On the west side of the courtyard was the entrance to the cross-hall. The central chamber would normally have had a subterranean strongroom like that at Chesters but the solid rock here made that impossible. Subsequently the building was altered. The porticoes in the courtyard were walled up, and traces of a late upper floor, and the remains of a heating system, found collapsed in the rear chambers suggest that an upper storey was installed at the back.

Hospital

The so-called hospital, behind the headquarters, was a simpler design and consisted of four wings of rooms around a central courtyard. The visible remains are of late date and lie over a smaller, Hadrianic, predecessor. The design was a conventional one though it is not associated here with any specific finds of surgical instruments. It may have had an upper floor: one or two of the 'rooms' are very narrow and may actually be staircase wells.

Commanding officer's house

Covering the largest area of all the buildings in the fort was the commanding officer's house. It resembles the hospital in plan but the steep hillside meant that it had to be terraced, not only for ease of construction, but also to let sunlight into the courtyard and rooms in the north wing. The surviving structure is of third-century date but in the north and west wings incorporated elements from its Hadrianic predecessor. A number of architectural features,

45   *The cross-hall of the Housesteads headquarters building looking south. At centre left are the remains of the steps into the hall from the courtyard. To the right is the range of rooms at the building's rear which contained the unit's standards and valuables. At the extreme centre right is the tribunal from which senior officers would have addressed soldiers of the garrison.*

such as fragments of columns, can be seen reused in the hypocaust in the north wing.

If Housesteads is still imposing in its ruined state, it was no less so in early modern times. The well-preserved ramparts made it an ideal base for brigands and cattle thieves. Camden was unable to approach in any safety about the beginning of the seventeenth century. He abandoned attempts to take measurements for fear of the 'rank robbers thereabouts'.

The walk west from Housesteads to Cawfields milecastle is the one section of Wall not to be missed under any circumstances. Leave the fort by the west gate which is the best preserved at the fort. By the end of the Roman period it had been blocked but this was cleared in modern times. Follow the western rampart up to where it meets the Wall which disappears into a small wood as it strikes west. This is one of the few stretches where it is possible to walk along the actual curtain. After a short distance the wood peters out and walkers must leave the Wall and take to the path beside it.

46   *The north gate of milecastle 37 looking north. Since this photograph was taken more arch stones have been replaced but undergrowth and a protective earth packing have largely obscured the lower parts of the massive masonry of the gate which can be seen clearly here. The door jamb on the far side of the gate can be seen leaning at an angle, either due to subsidence or as was once thought, deliberate demolition. At some time, probably in the third century, the gate was narrowed to a foot postern; the steep drop to the north made a full-sized gate here superfluous.*

Milecastle 37 (Housesteads West)

★★*Visible remains*★★: *milecastle (37) (Map 5). Free. OS Ref. NY 785687 (Sheet 87 1:50 000 Series; Sheet 546 1:25 000 Series).*

Only 0.3 mile (0.5km) west of Housesteads fort are the well-preserved remains of milecastle 37 (**46**). It was built by the II Legion *Augusta*, using Broad Wall measurements to begin with, under Aulus Platorius Nepos (Source 2). The change to Narrow Wall specifications may have come here before no more than the gates and footings of its walls had been constructed. With such a clearly-exposed plan, including footings of internal buildings, it's easy to see that the north-south dimension of the milecastle is shorter than the east-west, a type associated with the II Legion *Augusta*.

The outstanding remains of the north gate are built from massive blocks which stand slightly proud of the flanking walls, another feature of the II Legion's work. In this instance the gate's construction has clearly helped its survival for, alone among the milecastles, this one survives to the springers of the arch. Six are now in place but four of the blocks have been restored to their present positions in recent years. Subsidence seems to have been responsible for its partial collapse in Roman times. Its great value now is that, assuming the

Wall was originally higher than the arch in order to pass over it, then the Wall must have been at least 4.6m (15ft) high, but of course it could have been stepped up over. It is unknown if the substantial masonry of the gate was devised to support a tower, though it must have been strong enough to do so. An oddity about the north gate is that it is plain from taking a look through it to the north that it can have been of little use as a passage for trans-Wall traffic. This may have been why the gate was later narrowed, the blocking for which is still in place.

Walkers can skip the next two paragraphs which direct drivers to the next convenient stops.

Driving to Steel Rigg (or a detour to Vindolanda), and Cawfields

Those less keen on bracing walks (and a walk on the Wall can redefine the meaning of bracing under certain conditions) might like now to return to their cars or bicycles at Housesteads and head west for Steel Rigg (Peel Gap), or Cawfields. A good technique is to send a driver on to wait for walkers who wish to carry on to the west along the Wall. The road is particularly undulating and the dips show traces of innumerable scraped sumps for drivers who ignore the warning signs.

For Steel Rigg (Peel Gap) and Vindolanda return to the B6318 and head west for a little over 2.6 miles (4km) to Twice Brewed crossroads. If you wish to detour to Vindolanda now is a good time; if so, turn left (south) at the Twice Brewed crossroads and follow the directions in Chapter 8. For Steel Rigg turn right (north) instead and head towards the Wall. The minor road north to Steel Rigg leads to a National Trust car-park (fee payable) for visitors just north of the line of the Wall (NY 751677).

For Cawfields take the same route but keep going for a further 2.5 miles (4km) beyond to where a right turn (north) at the crossroads by Haltwhistle Burn takes vehicles to the Cawfields car-park.

HOTBANK MILECASTLE (38) *OS Ref. NY 772682*

For walkers from Housesteads this stretch of Wall is unforgettable. Strike out west from milecastle 37 for the site of milecastle 38 at Hotbank. Milecastle 38 becomes visible as the Wall proceeds down a gentle south-west-facing slope. Nowadays all that remains is a grassy mound, just beyond a dry-stone wall about halfway down. A pair of inscriptions (one broken) probably from here and similar to that from milecastle 37, but in better condition, have survived, recording that the II Legion *Augusta* built the milecastle during the reign of Hadrian and the governorship of Aulus Platorius Nepos (**3**; Source 2).

Just to the south of, and heading west parallel with, the Wall the *agger* of the Roman Military Way can be seen. Generally it was located between the Vallum and the Wall but tended to hug the latter wherever possible. This road must have been used as communications and supply link all the way along the Wall system but was not introduced until the late second century.

MILKING GAP *OS Ref. NY 771680*

Around 350m west of Hotbank milecastle a track runs south from the Wall through a narrow gap in the crags. This is known as 'Milking Gap' and is the site of one of several native settlements close to the Wall. Little is visible now but a short walk through the gap leads to a spot where mounds are visible on the right-hand (west) side of the gap (NY 772678). These are the remains of five stone round-houses and their enclosure wall. It was inevitable that the Wall and its systems would intrude on the habits and movements of local peoples. Indeed, the whole Wall system cuts across the tribal territory of the Brigantes.

CASTLE NICK MILECASTLE

Visible remains: *milecastle (39, 'Castle Nick') and Wall (Map 5). Free. OS Ref. NY 761677 (Sheet 87 1:50 000 Series; Sheet 546 1:25 000 Series).*

The walk to Castle Nick milecastle (39) leads along Highshield Crags above the waters of Crag Lough. The milecastle is so-called because of its location in a cut-out, or 'nick' in the hills. This is especially evident to those looking north from the B6318, at this point only around 500m to the south. Its position seems tactically disadvantageous, but there may have been other reasons for placing it here such as controlling passage through the gap.

The milecastle was built on Narrow Wall measurements but a Broad Wall foundation had been prepared along the north wall of the milecastle up to, and including, the gate. Nearby, excavations have shown that a stretch of the Wall foundations, prepared to Broad measurements, was unused and the new Narrow Wall erected on a different alignment. This illustrates how the Wall was being built in components when the order to change dimensions came. Unlike milecastle 37 Castle Nick's north-south dimension is longer than the east-west, and the gates lack monumental masonry (**47**), though they seem to have been narrowed in the late Roman period. It is unlikely that the II Legion was responsible for building it; no inscription has survived though the style is associated by some with the VI Legion. This raises the question mentioned earlier of whether milecastles had towers over their north gates. However, finds of window-glass near the north gate indicate that it did have a tower.

Recent work on the Wall just to the west of Castle Nick has shown that a very hard white lime mortar was applied lavishly during the building of the curtain. What is not certain is whether this was a deliberate attempt to make the Wall more prominent. It may have been devised to help protect the Wall from erosion, and would also have exposed damaged sections to patrols.

47   *Milecastle 39 (Castle Nick) looking east. Clearly built deliberately in a hollow, Castle Nick was of a different form to milecastle 37 (46) and lacks its colossal gate masonry. The steep drop to the north made a ditch superfluous here. In the distance (upper left) is Crag Lough; beyond, a clump of trees marks Hotbank and the site of milecastle 38.*

PEEL GAP TOWER

★★*Visible remains*★★: *tower foundations and Wall (Map 5). Free. OS Ref. NY 753675 (Sheet 87 1:50 000 Series; Sheet 546 1:25 000 Series).*

The climb out of Castle Nick's gap along Peel Crags is steep but the Wall has recently been consolidated here, and steps cut into the hillside. The observant walker will have noticed a remarkable dearth of turrets so far, despite the well-preserved nature of the rest of the structures. This is partly because many turrets were demolished during the Roman period, some as early as the late second century, and because much of the Wall itself was rebuilt from tumbled stones in the nineteenth century.

The walk down into Peel Gap is very steep, and involves negotiating a winding, narrow staircase cut into the rock. It is not recommended for small children or anyone unsure on their feet. In wet weather it is slippery and dangerous. In the gap, about 345m west of turret 39a, an extra turret, or tower, was found in 1986. It's easily visible to anyone climbing down the hill from the east. Thanks to the methodical system of turrets and milecastles the gap here turned out to be right in the middle of the stretch between turrets 39a and b. As it happens this stretch is also unusually long at a fraction over 700m or nearly half a Roman mile, instead of the theoretical one-third.

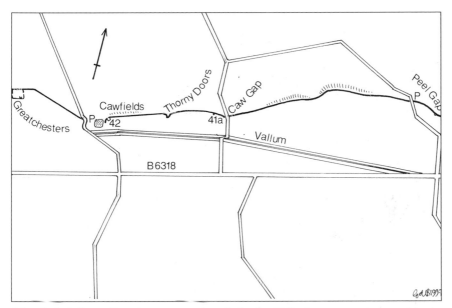

Map 6 *Peel Gap to Greatchesters, approximately 3 miles (5.8km) east to west (not to scale).*
P = *Parking.* **M** = *Museum. Turret 41a and milecastle 42.*

Conventional turrets were built with wing walls and later bonded into the curtain as it was built (but not in the western sector – see Chapter 6). The internal chambers were also recessed into the north wall of the turrets. Peel Gap tower has neither of these features and instead was built onto the back of the existing curtain. That it was a tower is only probable rather than certain; a platform beside it may have served as support for a ladder or wooden steps. A capstone from the site, and a whitewashed chamfered stone suggest that it had crenellations and that the Wall itself had a string course. It was probably built around the time the forts were introduced to the Wall system but, like most turrets, it was eventually demolished. In this case the pottery found is thought to suggest this took place no earlier than the first half of the third century.

The modern excavations on the site revealed some features hitherto unrecognized. On many sections of the Wall it has been shown that the Broad Wall foundation was built first, but subsequently the 'Narrow Wall' (very narrow in fact – no more than about 6 Roman feet wide) was placed on it, leaving an exposed section of foundation. At Peel Gap the Broad Wall seems to have been begun, but left incomplete for a period. During the intermission plant growth covered the unfinished Wall and had to be burnt off when construction resumed. This explains the burning found all over the Broad Wall foundation here but this is a theory rather than established fact. If correct, the theory suggests that there was a distinct hiatus in the Wall's construction when the dimension change came. Perhaps the builders were despatched to begin the forts at this point; it's a measure of how little we really know that no-one can say for sure.

85

48   *The Wall at Thorny Doors to the east of Cawfields milecastle looking south-east. As the Wall drops into the gap here it rises to 14 courses in height. The Vallum can just be seen below the clump of trees in the distance at upper right.*

Peel Gap is a good spot to return to the main road via Steel Rigg car-park for those who have walked enough for the day. The 2.75 mile (4.2km) walk on to Cawfields is a striking one along Winshields, the highest point on the Wall at 375m above sea-level, but apart from the Wall itself and the views there is less to see than up to this point. Walkers will reach the Caw Gap 1.5 miles (2.3km) west of Peel Gap. Here (NY 728668) the Wall drops into the narrow valley but diverts south on either side to a create a 'V'. This meant that anyone attempting to cross the Wall illegally was exposed to attack from all sides.

Turret 41a (NY 726669) is a clear example of a demolished turret. Here the south, east and west walls have all been reduced to their lower courses. Its recess was filled with blocks of which the lower three courses are in place. Behind, and above are the blocks of the original recess. For drivers the turret can be reached from the B6318 by turning right (north) at NY 727663 on a minor road which cuts the Wall at Caw Gap on its way to Edges Green. Turret 41a lies up a slope about 200m west of the minor road. Shortly beyond is Thorny Doors, another gap through the crags (NY 722668). At the bottom the Wall, pierced by a modern field gate, rises to a magnificent 14 courses and is one of the highest surviving stretches (**48**).

From here the walk down to Cawfields is along a gentle slope beside an impressive stretch of consolidated Wall. Due west on the opposite higher ground about 1 mile (1.6km) away a small clump of buildings marks the site of the fort at Greatchesters. Bruce warned in the 1800s that the house of Burn

49 *Milecastle 42 (Cawfields) looking north-east. Like milecastle 37 (**46**) the gates were built of substantial blocks. No internal structures have been identified here.*

Deviot to the north was a brigands' headquarters, and that lights seen at night in the house were 'the spirits of those who have been murdered in it'. Amusing now, it had more than a germ of truth in the 1800s.

Cawfields Milecastle

★★Visible remains**★★**: *milecastle (42) and Wall (Map 6). English Heritage. Free. Parking beside reservoir in old quarry. Access from B6318 via minor road, signposted Cawfields. OS Ref. NY 716667 (Sheet 87 1:50 000 Series; Sheet 546 1:25 000 Series).*

If arriving by road at Cawfields take a look to the west immediately after turning right from the B6318. Here the earthworks of earlier minor forts and camps can be spotted. Further along to the east the minor road crosses the Vallum (at NY 713665) which can be seen boldly striking across the low-lying land. Just to the west of the minor road, and opposite the entrance to the car-park is the site of the now-invisible Roman watermill at Haltwhistle Burn. A small peninsula created by a bend in the stream was exploited by cutting a channel across it, and building a weir. The concentrated flow of water would have turned a large vertical wooden wheel in the mill, uncovered here in 1907–8. The rotating shaft was harnessed to a mechanism for turning millstones, parts of which were found on the site. This demonstrates that the mill was engaged in food production, which can only have been for the benefit

50   *A reconstruction drawing of milecastle 42 based on **49**. The existence and form of the tower over the north gate is speculative as is the existence of the internal buildings. The Wall is shown with a patchy white rendering in accordance with recent discoveries, and without a parapet.*

of the Wall garrison.

Happily, Cawfields milecastle escaped the quarrying here which has now been stopped and an artificial lake created. In form the milecastle resembles that at Housesteads West (37) (**49**). It has similar proportions and heavy masonry for its gates, suggesting that it had a gate-tower (**50**). A tiny fragment of a Hadrianic building dedication stone, resembling those from numbers 37 and 38, was found here in 1848 (Source 2; **3**). Unfortunately, the legion's name is incomplete but the style of the milecastle suggests that the II Legion *Augusta* was responsible. A structural oddity here is that only the north wall of the milecastle and its north gate were built on Broad Wall measurements. The rest of the milecastle structure and the Wall on either side were built to Narrow measurements and abut the north wall without being bonded in. Unlike Housesteads Cawfields milecastle is not so well-preserved and there are no traces of internal buildings. This may be partly due to its being located on a steep slope.

Another inscription found here, this time on a tombstone but severely cut down in antiquity for reuse, might suggest that the milecastle was once manned by members of a Cohort of Pannonians (the unit's name does not survive in full). Such a unit is not testified at any of the Wall forts, though one is known at Beckfoot in Cumbria. A centurial stone from the vicinity names the Durotriges tribe from south-western Britain (**12**). This is not the only civilian unit testified on the Wall and it seems that at some stage, probably in the fourth century, it was necessary to bring in civilian labour from southern Britain to repair the Wall.

5. Cawfields to Birdoswald

GREATCHESTERS (*Aesica*)

Visible remains: *ramparts, and gates (Map 6). Private, footpath only through the middle of the fort. Best reached on foot from Cawfields milecastle car-park 700m to the east. OS Ref. NY 704668 (Sheet 86 or 87 1:50 000 Series; Sheet 546 1:25 000 Series).*

The Wall west from Cawfields is generally not as well-preserved as it is to the east. Farmhouses, out-buildings and field-walls have all taken their toll. To reach Greatchesters (also known as Great Chesters) leave the Cawfields car-park on foot and turn right (north) onto the minor road. Walk across the bridge over the stream where on the left is a stile over the field-wall and a footpath signpost labelled 'Pennine Way', and 'Great Chesters'. The path runs on the south side of the north-facing field wall, which stands on the course of the Wall, all the way up to the fort. Occasionally a short stretch of the lowest courses of the Roman Wall appear at the base of the field wall. The fort itself is marked by Greatchesters farm, and is in complete contrast to Housesteads. Part of the northern rampart is integrated into farm-buildings but the walls and two gates are reasonably visible.

At only 3.4 acres (1.4ha) Greatchesters is one of the smallest forts on the Wall. It is thought to have been a slightly later addition to the series because an inscription from outside the east gate bears Hadrian's name and a title which he was not awarded until the year 128. However, the inscription is very peculiar and can only suggest that building of some sort was probably still going on in that year or after and even that is uncertain (Source 5; **87**). It certainly doesn't mean that the fort was not *begun* after the others. The fort's name is something of a mystery too. It is thought to be a reference to a Celtic god called Esus, but as an adjective – or in other words something on the lines of 'The Esus place'. There may perhaps have been a temple, or before that a Celtic shrine, to the god.

Before the fort was built the site had already been allocated for milecastle 43

51   *The exposed section of vault of the headquarters building at Greatchesters (see the more complete version at Chesters, 28).*

which had been built on Broad Wall measurements. The fort was built just behind the Broad Wall and across the side walls of the milecastle which was then demolished along with the Broad Wall. The fort itself was built as one with the Narrow Wall on either side. Nevertheless, the fact that the Narrow Wall crosses the ends of external defensive ditches around the fort suggests that the sequence of activities was very rapid. Presumably the fort was planned and its ditches dug before the milecastle was demolished. In any case none of this is visible today.

The only internal building which can be seen is part of the vaulted strongroom of the headquarters building which still protrudes from the ground (**51**). An inscription found at the fort records that a granary was rebuilt under Severus Alexander in the year 225 (Source 18) but the structure has not been located. More interesting is the west gate which is the only fort gate on the whole Wall to retain its Roman blockings. A favourite habit of earlier excavators was systematic clearance of structures. They were anxious to expose the primary, usually Hadrianic, structures, to produce accurate ground-plans. Unfortunately, this meant that accumulations of fill and blockings, every one of which charted episodes in the fort's history, were removed for the understandable reason that they just looked like rubble. This gate escaped, and the blockings contrast with the more massive masonry of the footings of the gate-towers and piers. At least one displaced large block in the north carriageway fill suggests that the gate had been partially dismantled when it was blocked. Outside the fort to the west an unusually broad series of defensive ditches can be seen.

52   *Altar in the east gate-tower of the south gate at Greatchesters.*

The east guardroom in the denuded south gate contains an altar with a relief of a jug. This is one of the few carved objects which still stand *in situ* on the Wall (**52**). Nothing else of consequence can be seen but a *vicus*, containing a bath-house, spread out to the south of this gate.

The fort had an elaborate water-supply. An aqueduct was constructed to carry water from a point about 2.25 miles (3.6km) north but by taking maximum advantage of the natural landscape to lose height it covered a distance of 6 miles (10km). This wasn't a substantial stone or brick structure like the Pont du Gard in France, but instead a channel about 1m wide and deep which was cut into the hillside. Some of it can still be seen; the best means of tracing it is with the 1:25 000 Ordnance Survey map of the area (Pathfinder 546: Haltwhistle and Gilsland). Start at the fort and follow the thin dotted line which snakes away to the north-east, hugging the 210m contour, gradually climbing to 220m.

The Wall leaves Greatchesters at the north-west corner of the fort and continues on almost due west. It is no more than a grass-covered mound as it begins the climb up to Walltown Crags via Cockmount Hill. Modern dry-stone field-walls even cross the remains of the curtain with barely a hump acknowledging its denuded remains. The footpath runs up to 50m south of the Wall. Walkers can continue along here until they reach Walltown Crags in the vicinity of the remains of milecastle 45. The route takes in some features of

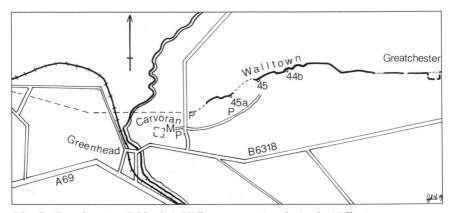

Map 7 *Greatchesters to Gilsland via Walltown, approximately 4 miles (6.5km) east to west (not to scale). **M** = Roman Army Museum. **P** = Parking. **44b** and **45a** = Turrets. (**45**) = Milecastle.*

interest. Milecastle 44 (NY 689669) is a conspicuous mound. At the site of turret 44b on Mucklebank Crags (NY 682668) the Wall turns a corner and as a result it forms the north and west walls of the turret.

If walking, now pass over the next section and carry on under the heading for Walltown Crags.

Driving from Cawfields to Carvoran

Drivers should return to Cawfields car-park and head back to the B6318, turning right (west). At a point 2.9 miles (4.75km) from here (NY 668655) turn right (north) to Walltown and the Stanegate fort of Carvoran (both signposted).

CARVORAN ROMAN ARMY MUSEUM

Museum (Vindolanda Trust) (Map 7). Open weekends from February to November, and all week March to October (closed December and January). Opens at 10.00 but late afternoon closing times vary, depending on the month. Entrance fee (with reduction if a joint ticket for Vindolanda entry is purchased). Tel: 016977–47485. Access from minor road leading north from B6318 (signposted). OS Ref. NY 667658 (Sheet 87 1:50 000 Series; Sheet 546 1:25 000).

The Roman Army Museum is part of the Vindolanda Trust organization. It lies by the north-east corner of the Stanegate fort of *Magnis*. The Museum is a monument to the Roman army and its role on the Wall and associated forts. There are many reconstructions, such as the inside of a barrack block and a large-scale model of the nearby fort, as well as artefacts from the Wall area. This is a useful place to visit in order to flesh out some of the ruined bare bones of

53 *The corn dry-measure from the fort at Carvoran. The name of the Emperor Domitian (81–96) has been erased but his titles remain. The stated capacity is 17.5 sextarii, a little over two gallons.*

the Wall and its forts, and will appeal particularly to children. A short film features actors portraying Roman military life on the Wall, including a centurion haranguing the audience. There is a tea-room, making the Museum a convenient place to escape from Wall wind and rain.

CARVORAN FORT (*Magnis*) OS Ref. NY 666656

The Stanegate fort at Carvoran, *Magnis* ('the Stones') is neither visitable, nor visible apart from the outline of its ramparts, thanks to the effects of eighteenth- and nineteenth-century agriculture. To see it, leave the Museum and turn left to walk down the track which runs beside the Museum building. From the field-gate the earth-covered north rampart can be clearly seen to the left (south).

Carvoran seems to have been built in stone in Hadrian's reign when the garrison was the First Cohort of Hamian archers (Sources 7 and 8). Finds from here include the corn measure now at Chesters (**53**). Carvoran had ambiguous status because it was not on the Wall but lay only some 300m away to the south beside the Stanegate. The Vallum skirted it to the north, specifically excluding it from the Wall 'zone' and implying the fort was already there, or at least planned when the Vallum was dug. So it would seem logical that the fort must

54   *The Wall at Walltown Crags from the south, west of turret 45a.*

have been originally of Trajanic, or earlier, date and belonging to the Stanegate chain of forts like Vindolanda. The trouble is that, to date, no evidence of any earlier fort has been found. On the other hand, it may have been felt that this was an instance where a fort was required to overlook the crossing of the Tipalt Burn 0.3 mile (0.5km) to the south-west; placing a fort on the Wall instead would certainly have been tactically disadvantageous. It was omitted from the Rudge cup (**7**) and Amiens skillet, which suggests it was not regarded as part of the Wall system.

Walltown Crags

★★*Visible remains*★★: *Wall and turrets (Map 7). English Heritage. Free. Access from minor road on B6318 leading to Carvoran Roman Army Museum (as above). OS Ref. NY 672662 to 683668 (Sheet 87 1:50 000 Series; Sheet 546 1:25 000 Series).*

Just opposite the entrance to Carvoran Roman Army Museum car-park is a metalled road leading eastwards up to Walltown Crags. Walk or drive up here to the car-park, just beyond a cattle grid. Now head on foot straight up the steep, grass-covered, hillside to reach a magnificent, and often-photographed, stretch of Wall where walkers from Greatchesters will eventually arrive. The crags are, or were, distinguished by a number of nicks known as the 'Nine Nicks of Thirlwall'. Quarrying has removed some of them, and the Wall too, but what remains has been consolidated to create the most splendid section of

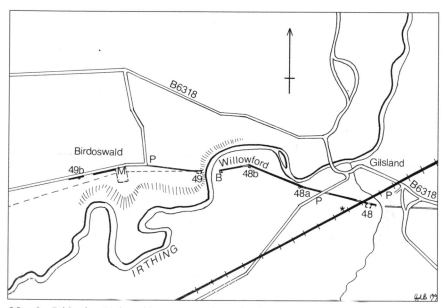

Map 8 *Gilsland to Birdoswald, approximately 1.75 miles (2.8km) east to west (not to scale).*
P = *Parking.* **M** = *Birdoswald site museum.* **48** = *Milecastle 48 (Poltross Burn).*
49 = *Milecastle 49 (Harrow's Scar).* **48a**, **48b**, *and* **49b** = *Turrets.* **B** = *Willowford Bridge abutment and mill races, and modern footbridge* ★ *marks the foot-crossing over the railway at Poltross Burn from where* **57** *was taken. The dotted line marks the course of the Turf Wall.*

curtain (**54**). For some of the stretch the Wall runs along a north-facing shelf below the crags simply because it would have been almost impossible to establish stable foundations on the bare rock above. The result must have been that any troops standing behind the Wall on the peaks would have had a better view to the north than anyone on the Wall itself. At one point the Wall negotiates a curved descent and here the builders splayed out the lower courses. This created a form of staircase, and may even have been used for access to the curtain.

Turret 45a, which lies a short walk to the east, appears to have been one of the several look-out towers constructed *prior* to the Wall (unlike those built *after*, like Peel Gap tower) and which were subsequently incorporated into the curtain. This is plain from the lack of wing walls which were normally an integral part of a Wall turret. The Wall meets, and leaves, the turret at an angle and is clearly of separate build. Even further east lie the remnants of milecastle 45. Nothing is visible, apart from the mound covering the ramparts, but a prominent scatter of blocks down the north-facing slope marks the debris of the milecastle's north wall, gate and tower(?). Walkers from Greatchesters will of course arrive here first.

To the west of Carvoran the Wall and Vallum are not in such a good state of preservation. Walkers can follow the line of the Wall past Holmhead (NY 659661), and then rejoin the footpath from the B6318 at NY 656661 beside a

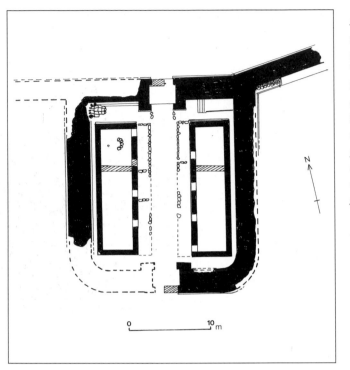

55   Plan of milecastle 48 (Poltross Burn). The milecastle had been severely damaged by the railway building and other robbing and the plan is thus partly restored. Later blockings in the gates and divisions in the barracks are shown hatched. (After F. Gerald Simpson.)

chunk of Wall high up on the west side of the road cutting. The spot is marked by a signpost labelled 'Hadrian's Wall', 'Wall End' and 'Chapel House'. From here walkers can head west past the site of milecastle 47, where a fragment of a Hadrianic building stone dedicated by the XX Legion was probably found (the only one known for this legion from a milecastle) and on to Gilsland. Watch out for the crossings cut through the Vallum mounds and the scattered piles of rubble still lying around.

Poltross Burn

★★*Visible remains*★★: *milecastle (48) and curtain (Map 8). English Heritage. Free. Access by footpath (200m) from car-park at Gilsland immediately west of the railway bridge. Follow signposts to Poltross Burn by turning sharp left immediately before railway bridge, then immediately right into Station Hotel car-park. OS Ref. NY 634662 (Sheet 86 1:50 000 Series; Sheet 546 1:25 000 Series).*

Drivers continue west on the B6318 from Carvoran, down the very steep hill into Greenhead, turning sharp right (north) just over the river bridge and following the road round to Gilsland. Just before Gilsland the main road turns right under a railway bridge: Poltross Burn is signposted left immediately *before* the railway bridge, and straight afterwards at a right turn into the Station Hotel

56   *The internal stairs at milecastle 48 (Poltross Burn) looking east. They suggest the mile-castle wall walkway was around 15ft (4.6m) high.*

car-park. The footpath to Poltross Burn leads from the far end of the car-park.

Milecastle 48 (Poltross Burn) escaped being totally destroyed by the adjacent railway which is just as well for it stands beside milecastle 37 (Housesteads) as one of the best-preserved, and thus most informative, of all milecastles (**55**). Located rather rakishly on an east-facing slope of an area of high ground between two streams, it now lies secreted in a small clearing reached by a footpath from the hotel car-park. The path leads to a footbridge over the burn, and then climbs extremely steeply up to the milecastle. On the way up the milecastle's Broad Wall east wing, and the flanking Broad Wall foundations are conspicuous, with a marked cut-in at the point the Narrow Wall abuts the wing (**5**).

No building inscription has ever been recovered from here, but the Broad Wall wings show that the milecastle was at least part-built by the time that the Wall was continued on the Narrow gauge. Inside are the remains of two barrack blocks, thought to have had an unusually large combined capacity of thirty or more, and ovens in the north-west corner. Rather more conspicuous is the flight of steps in the north-east corner. Assuming they once led to a walkway along around the milecastle ramparts then, restored, they suggest a height of about 3.7m (12ft) to 4.6m (15ft) depending on the lie of the land. But it is equally possible that the steps never ran to full height and instead only led to a platform on which a ladder was perched (**56**). Even if they did, this does not mean the height was matched elsewhere; these steps are exceptional and have not been found in other milecastles.

57 *The Wall at Gilsland, with the old vicarage at upper left, viewed from the railway embankment beside milecastle 48 (Poltross Burn).*

Walkers can continue along to the Wall at Willowford by following the footpath beside the railway line and crossing over a few metres south-west of the milecastle to head west. The footpath crosses a small valley at some distance from the Wall which runs along to the old Gilsland Vicarage (**57**) where, in spite of a rusty Ministry of Works sign, this stretch of Wall was apparently inaccessible in 1997, being fenced off with chicken-wire and surrounded by horses, sheep and various other animals. The footpath rejoins the line of the Wall at the next main road (NY 631663). From here the Wall is better preserved, and accessible, beside the path to Willowford. To get here by car from the Gilsland Station Hotel car-park involves a little reverse motion back down the path to the railway bridge. Turn left under it and carry on a short distance west along the B6318 into Gilsland. At the Give Way sign turn left for Willowford (signposted) and follow the road round to park in a lay-by just beside the school. This is where walkers from Poltross Burn will emerge.

Willowford

★★Visible remains★★: Wall, turrets (48a and b), bridge abutment (Map 8). Access from footpath on minor road south-west from Gilsland at OS Ref. NY 631663. Admission fee at Willowford Farm for the bridge, otherwise English Heritage and free, any time. Park in lay-by on south side of road. Distance from here to bridge abutment is about 0.6 mile (1km). OS Ref. NY 622665 (Sheet 86 1:50 000 Series; Sheet 546 1:25 000 Series).

58   *The end of the eastern sector of the Wall at Willowford bridge abutment looking south. In the centre are two sluices and to the right (west) is a channel, perhaps for a mill-race. The abutment was gradually extended as the river eroded its way west; the different styles of masonry are evident to the left of centre.*

The walk down to Willowford is by a footpath running just behind the well-preserved curtain. It leads through a working farm and is consequently fenced off. Scattered woodland just north of the Wall beside turret 48a would hardly have been permitted in ancient times and is a reminder that once out of the higher regions the land around the Wall, quite apart from the Wall itself, barely resembles its ancient appearance. Turret 48a, like the milecastle at Poltross Burn, has Broad Wall wings as does the less well-preserved turret 48b just beside the farm buildings further on. Broad Wall foundations are visible almost all the way down to the river. Note the centurial stone (marked with a plate) high up in the wall of one of the farm buildings by the path. At this point the Wall drops steeply into the valley of the Irthing. By the end of the path are the remains of the bridge abutment and channels for a water-mill.

The Irthing is steadily eroding its way west, and is thus some distance from its Roman channel. Consequently, the eastern bridge abutment is now high and dry, and the western abutment has disappeared. Even during the Roman period problems were caused by river movement. To begin with the Wall ended in a turret on the riverbank. On the north side the old Wall face is plain enough with small, squared stones. In a later phase the Wall was extended in much larger masonry, incorporating two culverts which were probably devised to control the flow of water through mill-races. Even this seems to have been inadequate, because the eastern culvert was subsequently blocked up by a new abutment on the south side. A much larger channel was created further west with the introduction of a substantial, separate pier (**58**). Excavation in the river valley here suggested that the river once flowed through a deep channel just beside the abutment; if so, then the hill opposite may have been less steep and the river deeper than they are now.

The modern footbridge from the Roman bridge abutment enclosure across the Irthing now allows walkers to make their way on to Birdoswald. However, the west bank is still a steep climb and in practice most visitors will wish to return to their cars and drive round. If so, return to the road at Gilsland, turn round and head west through Gilsland on the B6318 across the Irthing. Turn left (signposted for Birdoswald) just over the river. The Wall running down to Willowford can be glimpsed through the trees across the Irthing valley along the way. About 1.2 miles (2km) west a left turn at NY 615671 leads south to Birdoswald's crowded car-park (a recent introduction and not marked on all maps). The fort itself lies a little further on round the corner. As most people will visit the Wall between Birdoswald and the river from the former, that stretch is best described heading eastwards from Birdoswald rather than in the conventional westerly direction.

6. Birdoswald to Bowness-on-Solway

This chapter starts with the fort at Birdoswald but includes a description of the Wall *east* from here back to the Irthing opposite Willowford bridge abutment (see previous chapter). This is the most convenient way to visit that stretch of Wall.

BIRDOSWALD (*Banna*)

★★*Visible remains*★★: *fort, Wall, milecastle (49, Harrow's Scar) (Map 8). English Heritage. Entrance fee. Open 1 March to 30 November only, 10.00–5.30 (11.00–4.30 November, winter access to fort remains only). Tel: 01697–747602. Access on foot from the car-park on a minor road signposted south from the B6318 1.2 miles (2km) west of Gilsland. OS Ref. NY 615663 (Sheet 86 1:50 000 Series; Sheet 546 1:25 000 Series).*

Until recently Birdoswald was the site of a working farm. Modern excavations have thus been able to take advantage of relatively undisturbed remains, yielding some of the most valuable information to be recovered from the Wall. Pioneering environmental analysis has provided evidence for the landscape before and during the Roman period, while meticulous examination of internal structures has shown that the fort was inhabited long after the 'official' period of Roman rule in Britain.

The building of Birdoswald fort

From the Irthing west the Wall was built in its first phase out of turf with turf milecastles and stone turrets (timber turrets set into a turf wall would have subsided and collapsed). Pollen evidence suggests that when the Wall-builders arrived here they found dense woodland with a peat bog in the middle. The woodland occupied a narrow south-facing spur which looked out over a steep drop to the Irthing. The trees were cleared away and the Turf Wall, including

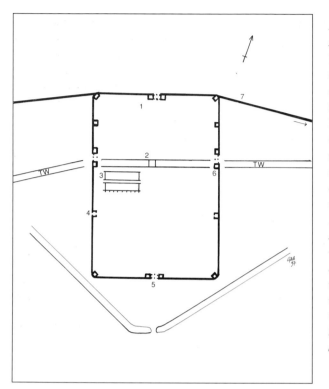

59   Plan of Birdoswald showing how the stone Wall was aligned with the north-west and north-east corners to bring the fort behind the Wall, instead of projecting north as it had done while the Turf Wall was in commission. **TW** *path of the Turf Wall (not visible).*

1 Entrance and museum. 2 Site of Turf Wall turret 49a (not visible). 3 Granaries and main west gate. 4 Southern west gate. 5 South gate. 6 East gate. 7 The Wall leading east to the milecastle at Harrow's Scar.

a stone turret (49a), was built here.

Shortly after the building of the Turf Wall here the Vallum was dug to the south, on the edge of the drop to the river. It diverted south to allow room for a fort but the fact that it was subsequently partly obscured by the fort's external ditch system suggests that a fort had already been decided on but not begun.

To make way for the fort the Turf Wall had to be demolished along with the stone turret. But it remained intact outside the fort, meeting it at the south towers of the east and west gates (**59**). This made Birdoswald, in its first phase, one of the projecting forts like Benwell or Chesters to the east. Consequently, like the other projecting forts, it had four main double gates, and two single-portalled gates. The Vallum was backfilled where it passed to the south. At 5.3 acres (2.2ha) Birdoswald was one of the bigger Wall forts. Examination of the pollen from the site has revealed that the fort was apparently left long enough, half-built, for scrub to grow over it. When construction resumed the scrub had to be burnt off (despite this, parts of the fort apparently remained unbuilt-upon throughout the rest of the second century).

Subsequently, and perhaps still during Hadrian's reign, the Turf Wall was rebuilt in stone from the Irthing past Birdoswald at least as far west as mile-castle 54. There is, however, no unequivocal evidence for this in the form of an inscription and it could have happened later. Instead of following the same line as the Turf Wall all the way, the new stone Wall diverted on either side of

Birdoswald to meet the fort's north-east and north-west corners instead of the main east and west gates (**59**). It thus no longer projected north of the line of the Wall. This made the single-portalled gates redundant and they were blocked up. The reason for the new Wall alignment may have been purely practical: it's plain to anyone walking round Birdoswald that land south of the Wall here is limited, thanks to the steep valley sides of the river. Moving the Wall line north made more protected land available close to the fort. The location gave the fort its name, *Banna*, a topographical term known in many forms usually applied to a promontory.

Visiting Birdoswald

The ramparts, four of the gates, and the two granaries are the most conspicuous remains. The north gate and much of the north-western part of the fort lie under the old farm buildings. Parts of the north wall, especially at the north-west corner, are visible by the main road.

Within the fort one of the old barns now serves as a museum and educational centre. It contains an instructive scale-model of the Wall in the vicinity and some finds from the fort, including the altar bearing the name of the *Venatores Banniess[es]*, the 'Hunters of Banna'. Although found at Birdoswald in 1821 the altar was long thought to refer to the outpost fort of Bewcastle, thanks to difficulties with interpreting the *Notitia Dignitatum* which appears to have a gap in its listing in this area.

Leave the museum and head out to the granaries and the west gate.

The granaries and the west gate

These have been the principal subject of excavations in recent years. An inscription from the fort, but reused in a barrack, records that a granary was built in 205–8 (Source 18). The inscription is important because it suggests that Birdoswald was being brought into full commission after protracted neglect; inscriptions from other forts in northern Britain suggests that this was part of a general policy of repair and rebuilding.

The paved flooring and substantial buttresses on the south side of each granary are well-preserved, especially on the southern example (**60**). They were of third-century date and one is thus probably that referred to in the inscription (Source 18). The flagstone floor was supported by piers, later joined up by sleeper walls. The buttresses were probably designed to support an overhanging roof (**78**).

The east and west gates were apparently repaired around the same time as the granaries were built. At the west gate ashlar masonry was used in its southern guard-chamber and sits oddly beside the smaller, cruder blocks normally used. If there was an ornamental or ceremonial purpose for this special stonework it has not been identified. However carefully the work was done the fort seems to have spent much of the third century allowed to decay

60   *The southern granary at Birdoswald looking south-west towards the western rampart.*

again. Another inscription, dated to 297–305, records that the commandant's house had been rebuilt from an earth-covered ruin, as had the headquarters building and a possible fort workshop or bath-house (Source 21).

Excavation of the granaries has shown that round the year 350 the north granary was partly dismantled to repair the southern one. While both had been in use for grain storage they were carefully maintained and, not surprisingly, there were few finds as a result. But in the fourth century the north granary collapsed and finds started to accumulate in the southern granary where a hearth was now installed. The spaces under the flagstone floor, between the sleeper walls, were filled with rubbish including rubble and late fourth-century pottery. Perhaps the south granary was now being used as a hall; at any rate occupation on the site continued long enough for a rectangular timber structure to be built on the foundations of the ruined north granary. Modern timbers mark the locations of the uprights which formed the structure of the hall. This new hall, and an adjacent building were erected on an alignment with the west gate.

One of the problems with post-Roman activity is that it is partly defined in archaeology by the lack of finds, such as coins and pottery. That makes the activity difficult to date – we can never know exactly what was going on here. It's quite possible that the fort was occupied by the descendants of the soldiers, using what they could of the old fortifications and buildings to create a secure home for themselves and their families. They may have had a leader, someone we might call a chief. Birdoswald raises the possibility that something like this was going on all along the old Wall. The length of time cannot be accurately

61 *The south gate at Birdoswald looking east. The conspicuous sills allowed the gates, pivoted in holes (visible on either side of the central jamb) to close hard up against them. This prevented anyone from levering them up.*

measured but it was long enough for the granaries eventually to collapse, followed by the building of the timber halls. This suggests that occupation here had continued long after the Roman period, and well into the fifth century.

In archaeological terms there is a conspicuous gap for most of the next thousand years (apart from an eighth-century Anglian brooch). By the thirteenth or fourteenth century there was a tower house on the site, and the old Roman west gate may have even formed part of the complex. Birdoswald was thus essentially a fortified farm, and the ruined fort provided a useful source of stone. In 1745 the present farmhouse was erected on the site.

The south gate

Leave the west gate and follow the ramparts around to the south gate, passing the single-portalled southern west gate, now unblocked. At the south gate pivot-holes for the wooden doors can be seen (**61**). The gate was entirely blocked up in the late Roman period, probably because its proximity to the steep hillside made it useless. Stand in the centre of the gate and look north across the fort. To the left the remains of the granaries and west gate can be seen in front of the later house with its crenellated tower. In the centre a distinctive mound marks the location of the largely-unexcavated headquarters building, and beneath it the Turf Wall's turret 49a. This area is plainly lower than the rest of the site and was an area of peat bog, identified by

62 Birdoswald east gate from outside the fort looking north. The north jamb of the north portal is one of the highest-standing sections of a gate on any fort on the Wall.

environmental analysis, when the Roman army arrived. To the right are the impressive remains of the east gate. Beyond, to the north and despite the trees, it's plain that Birdoswald commanded an impressive view. A beacon in the middle distance kept the garrison in touch with the fort at Bewcastle.

From here walk by the ramparts to the east gate, the best-preserved example on the Wall (**62**). Like the west gate it was built over the demolished Turf Wall and its infilled ditch. On the north side of the northern passage one of the door jambs still rises to one of the springers for an arch. This entrance was eventually converted into what is normally described as a 'guardroom' by blocking up the portals but only the blocking for the inside portal is still in position. Scattered nearby are some traces of the gate's superstructure, including window lintels, carved in arch-form. The reconstructed gate at South Shields (**86**) shows how these were used. An inscription of third-century date found nearby probably came from the gate (Source 20).

To the north of the east gate, and under the rampart piled up behind the stone wall, an arm-purse was found in 1949. It contained 28 silver coins (*denarii*) and was not deposited before the reign of Hadrian. It was probably dropped by someone working on the fort's original construction. Like many other finds from the site the hoard is now at Carlisle.

Recent survey work across the site has revealed a large *vicus* settlement to the east and west of the fort, leading to the suggestion that the Wall's civilian population may have been significantly underestimated.

*63   Centurial stone of Julius Primus of the VIII Cohort of an unspecified unit in the stretch
of Wall between Birdoswald and Harrow's Scar milecastle at about 250m west of the milecastle.
He may have been the Julius Primus on another centurial stone, from between Benwell and
Rudchester, and also on a tombstone erected to the wife of Julius Primus at Corbridge.*

EAST FROM BIRDOSWALD TO HARROW'S SCAR

★★*Visible remains*★★: *Wall, with centurial stones in situ (Map 8). Milecastle (49,
Harrow's Scar). English Heritage. Free. OS Ref. NY 620664 (milecastle) (Sheet 86
1:50 000 Series; Sheet 546 1:25 000 Series).*

Those who have crossed the Irthing at Willowford will have to follow this
route in reverse. Most people will find it more convenient to walk east from
Birdoswald towards the milecastle at Harrow's Scar. The Wall is visible from a
few metres east of the fort, just beside the sharp corner in the main road by the
car-park and signposted 'Harrow's Scar'. This is the only significant stretch of
stone Wall west of the Irthing which is visible today. The decision to rebuild in
stone here came after the introduction of the Narrow Wall to the east.
Consequently the stone Wall west of the Irthing is Narrow all the way and has
no Broad Wall foundation.

   Keep to the south to see one of the few stretches where the 'centurial stones'
placed in the stone curtain by the units responsible are still in place. They're
very difficult to find but modern small metal tags were placed in the Wall
below their positions (though in 1997 none of the tags appeared to be visible).
About 150m east from starting along the curtain is one of the clearest; it's in
the uppermost course (**63**). Another 54m or so along is a phallus but this is in

64   *Phallus in the Wall curtain east of Birdoswald.*

one of the lower courses and may be covered by undergrowth, depending on the time of year (**64**).

About 0.25 mile (0.4km) east of the fort is milecastle 49. It now stands at the top of the steep drop to the Irthing known as Harrow's Scar. In Roman times this was probably a gentler slope which soldiers and other traffic could make their way up. The milecastle isn't well-preserved but it makes for a sheltered stop. The Willowford bridge abutment can be glimpsed through the bushes and trees on the hillside. The Vallum ran up close to the milecastle's west wall but was terminated, instead of going round the milecastle. Clearly then it did not carry on down the hill, an unusual break in a feature of the Wall system which was normally dug regardless. The Turf Wall milecastle for this point was found to lie under the stone replacement but it was from here that the two Walls followed different courses until the site of milecastle 51 about 1.8 miles (2 Roman miles or 2.9km) west.

Now return to Birdoswald and resume the journey west.

From Birdoswald west the Wall is past its best though occasional features can be seen. It's certainly worth heading on a little way to see some of them. The road follows the line of the stone Wall, which is immediately beside and below the road. The Turf Wall diverts to the south here, and its route was followed by the Vallum. Not until a point 1.25 miles (2km) west of Birdoswald do the Turf and stone Walls converge. The British fleet had a hand in the stone Wall's construction here. Two of their centurial stones come from the Birdoswald area but their precise find spots are unknown. One is at Carlisle, the other is lost.

65   *The Turf Wall at High House looking south from the line of the stone Wall, west of Birdoswald. The prominent lower dark horizontal line is the forward ditch of the Turf Wall. Beyond is the Vallum ditch and mound system.*

THE TURF WALL AT HIGH HOUSE

Turret 49b can be seen about 320m west of Birdoswald (NY 612663) just to the south of the road (Map 8). There is nowhere to park and it is best reached on foot from Birdoswald. It was once in better shape; John Hodgson said that 'all of it in 1837 was taken away', though that was an exaggeration. This turret was on the part of the stone Wall which follows a different path to that of the Turf Wall. Unlike former Turf Wall turrets it was built as one with the stone Wall and is consequently fully bonded with it. Just beyond the turret the Wall peters out but the forward ditch, and the Vallum can be seen to the north and south respectively.

At NY 606660, about 0.6 mile (1km) west of the fort is the site of milecastle 50 (High House); 400m further on is a private track running south to High House itself (**65**). The track crosses the Turf Wall first and then the Vallum 180m south of the road; this is the only visible section of the Turf Wall, which is either entirely weathered away or now lies under the stone Wall. There's no access but if the light is good the mounds of the Turf Wall and Vallum can easily be seen from the main road. It also happens to be the site of the Turf Wall's milecastle 50 which is the only one on the Turf Wall to have escaped oblivion when the stone curtain was installed; the new stone milecastle was naturally located on the stone Wall to the north whereas at Harrow's Scar, for example, the Turf predecessor was found to lie under the stone replacement. Like the Wall it was built into, Turf

Wall milecastle 50 had turf ramparts. Remarkably, a fragment of a wooden dedication, similar to the stone examples from the stone milecastles to the east, was recovered here. Just enough survived to show that this Turf Wall milecastle was erected during Aulus Platorius Nepos' governorship under Hadrian, but not which unit or legion was responsible (Source 2).

All along here the Vallum is well-preserved. It diverts slightly to avoid Turf Wall milecastle 50, proving that the Turf Wall was still in commission when it was dug. Turrets 51a (Piper Sike; NY 588653) and 51b (Leahill; NY 584651) are both visible beside the road in this stretch, but on the north side. Parking at either is virtually impossible and motorists will have to make fleeting visits. Unlike turret 49b, these were originally built for the Turf Wall, and had to be integrated into the new stone Wall. Consequently they project slightly project north of the stone Wall and are not bonded with it. Milecastle 52 (Bankshead; NY 579649 – not visible) enclosed an exceptional 643 square metres which was more than twice normal – milecastle 37 for example enclosed 266 square metres. This was perhaps thanks to the long stretch of Wall between Birdoswald and the next fort at Castlesteads, itself detached from the Wall.

Now the Wall returns to the south side of the modern road.

PIKE HILL SIGNAL TOWER

Visible remains: *corner of pre-Wall observation tower. Access from Banks East turret lay-by (see below). English Heritage. Free. OS Ref. NY 577648 (Sheet 86 1:50 000 Series; Sheet 545 1:25 000 Series).*

Pike Hill signal tower, or what remains of it, was probably built under Trajan but later incorporated into the Wall (**66**). It's best reached from the parking spot for turret 52a (Banks East) down the slope about 100m to the west (see below). The Stanegate runs some way to the south here, across the Irthing, and a forward signal tower would have been an ideal means of keeping a watch to the north, and alerting troops at Nether Denton fort (not visible) on the Stanegate about a mile to the south-east across the river. That Pike Hill was not part of the original Wall system is self-evident from its orientation and the kink in the Wall which was necessary to incorporate it. Sadly, it was substantially demolished during nineteenth-century road workings and now only the south corner and entrance survive, immediately beside the road. An indent in the entrance probably held a timber door-jamb.

Banks East Turret

Visible remains: *turret (52a) and Wall. Footpath to Pike Hill tower. English Heritage. Free. Anytime. Park on lay-by on south side of the road. OS Ref. NY 575647 (Sheet 86 1:50 000 Series; Sheet 545 1:25 000 Series).*

66   *The sorry remains of Pike Hill signal tower. Most of the tower and the Wall in the vicinity have been destroyed. It faced north-west and the entrance (seen here) faced south-west. It was already standing when the Wall was built, and the latter had to be constructed in an awkward zig-zag to integrate the tower.*

67   *Turret 52a (Banks East) looking east. Pike Hill tower (**66**) stands at the high point in the distance to the right of the road. In the foreground a fragment of turret superstructure lies where it fell.*

The remains of turret 52a at Banks East are provided with a parking lay-by just to the east. A footpath leads east up to the Pike Hill signal tower (see above). The turret was originally constructed for the Turf Wall. Unusually, a large fragment of collapsed superstructure lies beside it but doesn't provide any conclusive evidence for the turret's original height or appearance (**67**). Note the neat course of chamfered levelling blocks in the north face of the turret a few courses above ground level.

Sadly, although the Wall once carried on here from to Bowness-on-Solway, there is practically nothing left visible, and what there is provides little of interest. The Vallum can be seen west of Banks East for more than a mile. A short, but impressively substantial, chunk of Wall at Hare Hill (NY 564646) is in fact largely rebuilt and only the bottom couple of courses are Roman. From the site of milecastle 54 (NY 551645) the Wall was built of friable red sandstone, not the harder limestone used to the east. It has eroded to a far greater extent, quite apart from being robbed out for building. Thus, from hereon the curtain can be regarded as being effectively invisible, apart from fragments. A short stretch covered in turf for protection can be seen on the west side of the stream at Dovecote (NY 526644) about one-third of a mile (0.5km) east of Walton, reached by minor roads from Banks and Lanercost. Those who wish to visit Bewcastle and its limited remains should turn to Chapter 7 for directions from the village of Banks here on the Wall.

CASTLESTEADS (*Camboglanna*) OS Ref. NY 512635

Castlesteads was destroyed in the late eighteenth century when a country house was erected on the site, though erosion from the river has also removed part of the platform; appropriately enough the ancient name seems to mean 'the bank on the bend [in the river]'. Nothing can now be seen of the fort but it's worth mentioning because, exceptionally, the fort lies between the Wall and Vallum rather than on or by the Wall itself which lies a quarter of a mile (0.4km) to the north-west across a stream called the Cam Beck. This indicates that it was officially regarded as being in the Wall system, and explains why its name appears on the Rudge Cup (**7**).

VEX·LIEG· ⅡⅠ∧VG·OF·∧PR·
SVB·∧GRICOL∧·OPTIONE

68 **a** *One of the inscriptions on the Written Rock of Gelt in a Roman quarry (after Collingwood and Wright).* **b** *The inscription is barely legible (see text) but the X of VEX can be seen (arrowed).*

STANWIX (*Uxelodunum* or *Petrianis*) OS Ref. NY 401571

Stanwix lies across the river Eden to the north of Carlisle. The fort here not only guarded the crossing but was also the biggest fort on the Wall at more than 9.3 acres (3.7ha). Its size makes it as good as certain that this was the home of the only thousand-strong (*milliaria*) cavalry unit in the province of Britain, the Ala Petriana, and thus the headquarters of the Wall system. Its Roman name is a problem. The Rudge Cup (**7**) supplies *Uxelodunum* ('High Fort') for the next fort west from Castlesteads but this has not been confirmed by an inscription from Stanwix. The *Notitia Dignitatum* calls it the *Ala Petriana* at *Petrianis* which is either a mistake, or else the fort had come to be known by that of its unit. Unfortunately the fort has been almost entirely obscured by modern Stanwix. Some of the south rampart is theoretically visible in the churchyard by Brampton Road (B6264; at NY 401571) but in practice is undetectable in the undergrowth. The only visible relic of the fort is a fragment of the north wall. To see it follow the A7 main road north through Stanwix (Scotland Road) past the Cumbria Park Hotel, and turn right (east) up Mulcaster Court. The fragment is in the far corner of the hotel car-park in a little brick enclosure, but consists only of wall core and three chamfered blocks from the front of the base.

THE WRITTEN ROCK OF GELT OS Ref. NY 526587

All along the Wall zone are scattered quarries, many of which were worked in Roman times for the Wall. One of the more remarkable is near Gelt. It's not too difficult to find. The A689 skirts Brampton to the south. Leave it and head south on the A69 for half a mile (0.8km) south where it crosses the river Gelt at Gelt Side. A minor road heads east to Low Geltbridge. On the corner where this road turns to the south a footpath heads south-east along the north side of the river Gelt. Walk along here for about half a mile (0.8km) until a concrete embankment appears; climb the narrow steps and continue walking for about 30ft (9m). At this point some 8ft (2.5m) above are the weathered rock-cut inscriptions left by the Roman masons. They are now very difficult to read. Probably the most easily seen is the letter **x**, from a now barely-legible inscription, just above a sharp v-shaped cut into the rock (**68**). It refers to the presence of one Apr[ilis?] from a vexillation of II Legion *Augusta* under the command of an *optio* (next in seniority after a centurion) called Agricola. However, the rock here flakes easily and, not surprisingly, it has all but weathered away. Several other inscriptions were once visible immediately to the right. Note the sections of rock face with tooling marks where blocks were chipped away, one by one, before being removed to the Wall probably by water down the Gelt to where it joined the Irthing. The Rock of Gelt is fun to find but not easy – there's more satisfaction to be had in locating it than anything learned.

CARLISLE

Museum at Carlisle Public Library and Art Gallery in Tullie House, Castle Street. Open all year round 10.00–5.00 (Monday to Saturday), 12.00–5.00 (Sunday). Entrance fee (half-price between 10.00 and 11.00, and free to members of the National Arts Collection Fund). Tel: 01228–534781 (museum) and 512444 (Tourist Information Centre). In central Carlisle between the castle and cathedral in a square formed by Annetwell Street, Castle Street, Paternoster Row and Abbey Street. Best reached by foot from one of the car-parks by the A595 as much of central Carlisle is pedestrianized.

Tullie House was built in the late 1600s but includes within its grounds the remains of a third-century shrine, the only visible part of Roman *Luguvalium*. The newly-expanded and renovated museum contains scenes of Roman life in the area including a reconstructed Roman street, and a stretch of Turf Wall, replete with replica *cheiroballista* (small catapult) and push-button sound effect. Other finds on display include centurial stones from the Wall and many altars and reliefs from forts in the area such as Bewcastle and Netherby (see Chapter 8). Carlisle has also turned out (like Vindolanda) to have waterlogged deposits which have produced wooden writing tablets, one stating evocatively 'IN BRITAN[N]IA'.

Carlisle was a Stanegate fort from the late first century until about the year 105 when it was demolished. Its garrison then may have been the *Ala Petriana*, named on a fragmentary inscription from here, and later based at Stanwix over the river on the Wall. Carlisle then developed into a town and, along with Corbridge, became one of the very few major civilian settlements a short distance from the Wall. It must have been inextricably linked, socially and economically, with the frontier garrisons, resembling a military town like Aldershot.

After the fort at Stanwix the Wall crossed the Eden over a bridge, the ruins of which were still visible in the sixteenth century. Blocks dredged from the river, and believed to be from the Roman bridge, are displayed in an enclosure on the south bank in Bitts Park (NY 395567).

Those who wish to visit the fort at Birrens and siege works at Burnswark should leave the Wall area by the A74 north from Carlisle and turn to Chapter 7 for directions. To trace the Wall west from Carlisle, head south-west from the city centre on the A595 for about 400m, and take the right fork (west) onto the B5307. Take another right fork 1 mile (1.6km) further at Belle Vue onto a minor road which leads to Burgh by Sands via Kirkandrews-on-Eden. The road does not follow the Wall precisely but from Burgh onwards it corresponds well enough.

BURGH BY SANDS (Aballava) *OS Ref. NY 328592*

The Wall headed west towards the forts at Burgh by Sands, Drumburgh, and Bowness. The Wall followed the south bank of the river more closely than the Vallum which pursued a more straight-line course across slightly higher ground. The 4.9-acre (2ha) fort at Burgh (poetically called *Aballava*, 'the apple orchard') now lies beneath the village. An earlier nearby timber fort, of either Trajanic or early Hadrianic date and probably associated with the Stanegate, has been located from the air. It overlies an even earlier timber watchtower. Excavations have suggested that the Vallum might run under the stone fort, as at Carrawburgh.

Nothing is visible but it's worth taking a look at the castle-like church of St Michael's which was built almost entirely out of stones taken from the Wall and fort. Although this might seem to be a very different use of the masonry this was once a dangerous area with continual border skirmishes. That the church looks like a miniature castle is no coincidence.

Recent excavations to the west of Burgh have showed that parts of the Turf Wall here were built on a 4.8m (19ft) wide foundation made of cobblestones. This was unusual – normally the turfs were laid straight onto subsoil, but cobble foundations were frequently used in forts with turf and timber ramparts.

DRUMBURGH (*Concavata*) *OS Ref. NY 265598*

Beyond Burgh the Wall dropped down to the low-lying land on the south bank of the Solway Firth. Running the Wall along here was essential because at very low tide it was, and still is, possible to wade and swim over from Scotland. The Wall hugged the southern shore. The fort at Drumburgh 4 miles (6km) west of Burgh, was very small at 2 acres (0.8ha), and began life as a turf fort attached to the Turf Wall. The meaning of its ancient name is unknown. It seems to have been rebuilt in stone but on an even smaller scale. The road follows much of the Wall's meandering route to Bowness from here but the Vallum steered a much more direct course.

At NY 244617 it's possible to see some of the Vallum, just south of the village of Port Carlisle. It sat to the rear of turret 78a itself, like the Wall, no longer visible. The Wall was destroyed here only in the nineteenth century, having survived to a significant height.

BOWNESS–ON–SOLWAY (*Maia*) *OS Ref. NY 223627*

The Wall terminated at Bowness. The village's main road runs straight through the middle of the 7-acre (2.8ha) fort, almost on the alignment of its east and west gates. Nothing can now be seen though the fort's ramparts have been traced by piecemeal excavation. The northern rampart has been eroded away by the sea. Beyond the fort the Wall ran down into the sea.

Bowness was not the end of the Roman frontier. The milecastles and turrets, probably connected by a wooden palisade, were continued down the Cumbrian coast. They are now called milefortlets and towers to distinguish them from the Wall system. Unlike the Tyne estuary in the east, the Solway Firth forms a huge cut into the western coast of Britain but was not so wide, or deep, that it prevents fording at low water. The chain of defences ran all the way along the coast past forts at Beckfoot and Maryport, and were backed up at a network of forts in northern Britain.

Little is visible at any of these places, but the following are of interest:

SWARTHY HILL/CROSSCANONBY MILEFORTLET *OS Ref. NY 067399*

The consolidated turf ramparts and ditch are visible on on inland-facing slope behind the B5300 2 miles (3.2km) north-east of Maryport.

MARYPORT *OS Ref. NY 037373*

Senhouse Roman Museum, The Battery, The Promenade at the north-east extremity of the town. Admission charge. Tel: 01900–816168 – open all year (all week July–September; Tuesday, Thursday–Sunday and Bank Holidays April–June and October; Friday–Sunday only from November to March. Open 10.00–5.00 April–October, 10.30–4.00 November to March).

The Museum contains stones from the fort, including some of the annually-renewed dedication altars to Jupiter Optimus Maximus by the First Cohort of Spaniards. The fort (*Alauna*, 'Shining') is not accessible.

7. Outpost forts

Rome regarded the land beyond the Wall as hers too, but as a more expendable commodity. In this respect it served as a buffer; this was where Roman influence and power was diffused into territory in the far north. So, the Roman army constructed forts in this zone. Some were erected on the sites of forts constructed in the late first century, and re-used during the period of the Antonine Wall where they functioned as hinterland forts to that short-lived frontier. Others were new foundations. Generally they were similar to the forts on the Wall in size and garrison but instead they guarded roads. Some of these forts are worth visiting today. None is properly consolidated or in the guardianship of English Heritage, and local permission from landowners is normally required.

An itinerary of outpost forts as a day's trip is impractical. Instead, they can be visited as major detours from the Wall, or as part of longer journeys into Scotland itself. Risingham and High Rochester are relatively close to one another, as are Birrens and Bewcastle. So the order here is of no particular significance. Unfortunately they are all only really visitable by independent transport. Be warned though: the A68 is a challenging road with a series of rapid steep climbs and drops.

MARCHING CAMP AT COCK PLAY (SWINE HILL) *OS Ref. NY 905825*

The A68 out of Corbridge crosses the Wall at Port Gate and then strikes ahead on the line of Roman Dere Street into what was once the wilderness of northern Britain. Way out here are the remote forts of Risingham and High Rochester. The whole area is scattered with the remains of earthworks of the Roman army's temporary camps and many can be traced by following the Ordnance Survey map. One on the way to Risingham is easily found by the A68 at Cock Play/Fourlaws. Here the A68 diverts from Roman Dere Street by turning sharply to the right (north-east). On the left of the road here a footpath heads south-west across a camp of indeterminate Roman date. This kind of

69   All that remains of 'Rob of Risingham', a Romano-British warrior god and perhaps the one known as Mars-Cocidius. Originally about 1m in height. Near to the fort at Risingham.

fortification could have been thrown up in a matter of hours to protect a unit on campaign for a night or more. The north entrance is the best preserved. On the north the rampart is broken and one side swings into the fort to create a staggered entrance. This obliged a would-be attacker to walk down a fortified corridor.

ROB OF RISINGHAM

Visible remains: *lower part of relief of warrior god, probably Mars-Cocidius. Access by track from the A68 at Broomhill. Turn left (for those heading north) at NY 899859 and follow the track as it curves round to the south towards Parkhead quarry. The relief is visible on the left (east) side up the slope. OS Ref. NY 899858 (Sheet 80 1:50 000 Series).*

In the military zone the most popular deities were warrior and hunter gods. One of these was known as Cocidius, usually combined with Mars to create a classical and British hybrid. Such gods were usually worshipped at small rural open-air shrines. A carving of one survives at Risingham. In the early nineteenth century the so-called 'Rob of Risingham' consisted of a figure carved in relief wearing a military-style tunic, a quiver, wielding a bow and carrying a small bag. A panel above seems to have been intended for an inscription. This was almost certainly a depiction of Mars-Cocidius but tragically the farmer here became entirely sick of visitors tramping across his land to see the curious figure and smashed it up. He stopped half-way through the job and, thankfully, the lower half of Rob remains intact (**69**). It isn't difficult to find and the figure's legs, left arm and bag, and lower part of his tunic can be seen. Many other types of rural shrine are known in the military zone but are often only marked by occasional finds of altars.

RISINGHAM (*Habitancum*)

Visible remains: *fort platform and buried ramparts. Private land, seek permission at farm. Scattered stonework but nothing substantial. Access from the A68 on a track (gated) heading west (turn left if coming from the south as the A68 comes down a steep slope into West Woodburn), opposite the turning to East Woodburn. OS Ref. NY 890863 (Sheet 80 1:50 000 Series).*

Risingham fort is on private ground and permission is needed from the farm here in order to walk over it. *Habitancum*, named only on an altar, may mean 'The Estate of Habitus', an unknown individual. It lies in a north-facing gap in the hills on the south side of the river Rede. Built on a low rise in the gap the platform is very prominent, though it must be stressed that there is really nothing else to see here now apart from the location.

Despite the lack of visible remains on site Risingham has yielded some remarkable inscriptions. One now at Trinity College, Cambridge, was dedicated to the divine powers of more than one emperor by the Fourth mounted Cohort of Gauls, a unit which is also testified at Vindolanda (**81**). That more than one emperor is indicated by the inscription means that a period of joint rule must be referred to. The style of the inscription is later second century so this suggests that it belongs to Marcus Aurelius' period of joint rule with his intended heir Lucius Verus, 161–9, or then with his son Commodus, 177–92. However, little else is known of the second-century fort which was probably built, like that at High Rochester, in the 140s. It stood long enough for parts to fall down by the early third century. An inscription from the south gate records that the First mounted milliary Cohort of Vangiones was responsible for its rebuilding between 205–7 (Source 18). It was a substantial single-portalled gate with projecting towers which resemble rather later Roman military architecture. The north gate is now robbed away, no east gate is known, and the west gate was a fourth-century addition. The Vangiones seem to have shared the garrison with a unit of pikemen from Raetia and another of scouts. All three units are mentioned on a fragmentary inscription from here of 213 now at Newcastle.

HIGH ROCHESTER (*Bremenium*)

★★*Visible remains*★★: *fort ramparts, west and north gates, Roman road (Dere Street) and roadside tomb. Private. Seek permission at farm on fort platform. Access is from the A696 2.5 miles (4km) north of the junction with the A68 as it heads north from Corbridge and the Wall at Port Gate. A minor road forks right from the A696 and leads up to the fort platform 0.6 mile (1km) to the north from the main road. The fork is marked by a house between main and minor road with a distinctive porch constructed of Roman gutter stones, an arch, and finials made of large round boulders (Roman catapult ammunition). OS Ref. NY 833987 (Sheet 80 1:50 000 Series).*

High Rochester (*Bremenium* – 'roaring stream') is a Roman fort on Dere Street, followed mostly by the A68 and some of the A696 but here the Roman road takes to higher ground. The fort lies between the modern main road and the Roman road to the east. The fort platform is now a farm but remains largely open with farm buildings scattered around its ramparts on the north and west sides. It commands sensational views to the south, west and north and makes an invigorating place to visit.

Although High Rochester was partly excavated in the mid-nineteenth century, apart from the ramparts and gates, little stands above ground today. There was a fort here in the late first century but it remained unoccupied thereafter until the time of the building of the Antonine Wall, when it was garrisoned by the First mounted Cohort of Lingones. An unusually complete and specific inscription from the site commemorates their presence during the governorship of Lollius Urbicus (c. 138–42 – see Source 9). Out here in the barren countryside a cavalry unit of some sort would have been essential if the territory. Once the withdrawal from the Antonine Wall was completed in the 160s High Rochester remained in use, and seems eventually to have been utilized for a specific application. An inscription from the year 220 in the reign of Elagabalus records the building or restoration of a *ballistarium* 'from the ground up'; another from the reign of Severus Alexander (221–35) says the same (Sources 18 and 21). They imply that the *ballistarium*, an installation associated with artillery, had been there for long enough to need repair perhaps since the time the Antonine Wall was given up, though it is also possible that the wars in the 170s and 180s made it necessary to build up High Rochester's defences.

The road leads into the fort across the south gate. Ask at the farm for permission to walk round. The fourth-century west gate is the best-preserved part of the fort today. Take the track which heads out and through the west rampart, turn right (north) and walk along the outside of the rampart to the west gate. The huge Roman blocks are easily distinguished from the modern field-wall on the earth rampart behind (**70**). The gate is blocked now but the north springer for the single arch is quite evident. Now follow the rampart round to the north and look out across the landscape. Dere Street can be seen as a low ridge coming up from behind and past the fort to the east. Just beyond

70 *The west gate at High Rochester. The large blocks are the Roman masonry; the blocking and field wall on top of the rampart are modern. The moulded block marks the point where the arch for the single-portalled entrance rose from. Mid-second century or later.*

the site of the north gate the ground drops away sharply to the steep valley of the 'rushing stream' which gave the fort its name.

The most unusual sight at High Rochester is a roadside Roman tomb. Burial outside the walls of a settlement was required by Roman law on the grounds of hygiene. In Britain only a few Roman tombs are visible today. At High Rochester however the lower courses of one monumental circular tomb still stand alongside Dere Street to the south-west of the fort. Getting there involves crossing fences and fields to cover the odd half-mile or so. It's best to ask directions from the farm but almost any route due south-east will take the walker to the very-conspicuous ridge of Dere Street. Head along it until a low rotunda of stone blocks appears to the west of the road (**71**). This is the lower part of a tomb which will once have stood very much higher, perhaps 5m (16ft), and was probably capped by a cone made of turf or stone. Walk round it and look for the head of a wild animal carved in low relief on one of the blocks. The occupant of the tomb, who had been cremated and buried with a coin of Severus Alexander, is unknown but is likely to have been a senior officer from the fort, perhaps one of the prefects. It was one of several stone tombs in the immediate vicinity but the blocks from the others have all been reused elsewhere.

Perhaps the most intriguing find from High Rochester is the carving of a pair of water nymphs attending Venus bathing (now at Newcastle). The sculptor was evidently familiar with the subject matter and had presumably been

71   *A Roman tomb beside the Roman road of Dere Street as it heads north past the fort of High Rochester. The fort, marked by the clump of trees at upper left, is about half a mile (0.9km) away.*

commissioned to produce a well-known mythological scene. What makes it interesting is that this is not so much an instance of a classical scene depicted in provincial 'Celtic' style (which was often highly accomplished) as just, simply, a poor piece of work. The sculptor has clearly attempted to reproduce faithfully the iconography of classical form and composition but it was beyond him (**72**).

BEWCASTLE (*Fanum Cocidii*)

★★Visible remains**★★***: fort rampart. From Banks, on the Wall west of Birdoswald, take the minor road north and head on over the B6318; bear right a mile later and keep going past Askerton Castle. After this point the drive becomes more challenging and eventually winds down into Bewcastle. OS Ref. NY 565747 (Sheet 85 1:50 000 Series).*

Bewcastle's Roman name, *Fanum Cocidii* ('The Temple of Cocidius'), is one of the few whose meaning is not in doubt. In Roman times it was reached by a road which struck out north-west from the north gate of Birdoswald fort on the Wall 6 miles (10km) away. On the road a signal station at Gillalees Beacon (NY 579718) maintained a line of visual communication over the high ground which separates the two forts. Unfortunately access today is nothing like so straightforward: the old road has barely made an impact on modern routes.

72   *Carved relief from High Rochester depicting Venus being attended by two hand-maidens. Note the head of a bearded god at upper left. Third century. Height 0.67m.*

Bewcastle occupies a small area of high ground in the valley of the Kirk Beck. The fort seems to have been built under Hadrian but that assertion is based on the report of a long-lost inscription naming him and the II and XX Legions (Source 6), and the style of the bath-house. Unusually for a bath-house it ended up (if it wasn't already) within the fort ramparts thanks to the pragmatic Roman approach to the irregular site. Contrary to popular belief the regimented Roman fort plan was often adapted to local conditions and Bewcastle is one such case. The known ramparts belong to the early third century and follow an irregular hexagonal plan. A Norman castle occupies the north-east corner. Some of the internal buildings have been examined and were generally conventional in plan. Inside the headquarters' strongroom were two curious plaques to the god Cocidius (**73**). Altars from the fort also mention *Sancto Cocidio* ('to Holy Cocidius') and 'Imperial Discipline' (**74**). The name of the fort makes this hardly surprising but exactly where his shrine or temple was is unknown. The finds mentioning him are now at Carlisle. The building seems to have burnt down during the late third century. During the fourth century there were at least two more phases of rebuilding here, the second of which involved reconstructing the fort walls.

Little else is known about Bewcastle. Only the south-west rampart is at all conspicuous today. The Norman keep is partly built of Roman masonry. Rather more striking than either is the churchyard's seventh- or eighth-century Bewcastle Cross, or at any rate its shaft, which still stands to 4.4m (16ft) in height and depicts Christ, St John the Baptist, and St John the Evangelist. It also carries more abstract decoration and a poem written in runes.

73   *Silver plaque dedicated 'to the God Cocidius', and found in the underground strongroom of the fort at Bewcastle. Third century. Height 110mm.*

The presence of an object like this illustrates the existence of an early church foundation here. It was not uncommon for early Christian sites to develop in or around the sites of Roman temples, something which has been demonstrated archaeologically at several sites in southern Britain, for example at Uley in Gloucestershire. This came about not just as a consequence of continuing to gather in traditional places but also out of a desire on the part of the church to exploit such habits. This may well have been the case here too, building on a long-established tradition of Bewcastle as a religious centre of local importance.

BIRRENS (*Blatovulgium*)

★★*Visible remains*★★: *fort ramparts. On private farmland. Easily accessible by road. Head north on the A74 from Carlisle past Gretna Green into Scotland. Leave on the B722 exit turning right (north-east) towards Eaglesfield. Immediately after the junction the B722 crosses a railway cutting and just past this is a left turn heading north-west. Follow this for a little over a mile (1.6km). The fort is visible to the left (west) between the road and the railway now on an embankment. OS Ref. NY 218752 (Sheet 85 1:50 000 Series).*

74 *The archaeologist F. Gerald Simpson at Bewcastle displaying an altar dedicated to Imperial Discipline found during excavation of the head-quarters building in 1937. (Courtesy of Dr Grace Simpson.)*

The fort at Birrens (*Blatovulgium* – apparently either a 'flowery hillock' or a 'flour-sack') lies almost due north of Bowness-on-Solway, but on the Scottish side of the water. Birrens served a crucial strategic purpose by guarding approaches to the western end of the Wall by land, and across the Solway Firth. It also commanded the north-western route into Scotland. Most of the fort platform is visible but the southern part has been eroded away by the stream which flows past it. It began life in the late first century on a smaller scale, but was rebuilt under Hadrian and then again during the period of the Antonine Wall when it was consolidated in stone at 4.9 acres (2ha) in size. It has been extensively excavated and was shown to have lasted only a short time before it was destroyed by fire. It was rebuilt once more, by the Second Cohort of Tungrians(?) in the year 158 (Source 9).

Unlike High Rochester and Bewcastle the fort here did not outlive the second century and was eventually abandoned, perhaps as soon as the 180s. At the site today the only visible remains apart from the platform are the numerous ditches and mounds which formed the northern defences of the fort. They aren't particularly exciting but the detour here is worth making in order to carry on and see the magnificent siege works at Burnswark.

75   *The Roman practice siege camp at Burnswark looking north-east. The mounds were catapult emplacements.*

Burnswark

★★*Visible remains*★★: *Roman siege earthworks. Access is as for Birrens (above) first. From Birrens continue north into Middlebie and turn left onto the B725 and head south-west for 1.25 miles (2km). Here the main road turns sharp left. On the corner here turn right up the minor road (crossing a railway on the A725 means the turning has been missed) for 2 miles (3.2km). Eventually the road curves to the right (north-east) in front of a small area of conifer forest. The eastern edge of the forest marks the eastern rampart of a huge Roman camp at the foot of rocky hill on which is an Iron-Age hill-fort. OS Ref. NY 188785 (Sheet 85 1:50 000 Series).*

The spectacular Roman earthworks here reputedly belong rather vaguely to some time after the late second century. It is probable that this was a practice fort because the hill-fort seems not to have been occupied at the same time. The earthworks consist of a large, approximately rectangular, rampart. On the south, east, and west sides the rampart is broken with a small section of rampart outside the break. This is a *titulum*, or common Roman earthwork defensive gateway. On the north rampart are three extremely prominent mounds: one at each corner, and one in the middle. The ditch around each mound was from where the earth was thrown up to create the mound (**75**). These were platforms for catapults, *onagri*, which consisted of wooden frames and a large arm with ammunition in a cup at one end. The arm was mounted on a shaft which had twisted ropes on either side. By cranking the arm down the ropes

127

became twisted and held enough force to hurl large boulders in the cup at the end of the arm some distance. Lead sling-bolts found hereabouts show that catapult firing was not the only activity.

The other major outpost fort in the west was at Netherby, *Castra Exploratorum* ('Camp of the Scouts' – once thought to have been *Uxelodunum* but this name is now confidently attributed to Stanwix on the Wall). The fort has long since been built over, first by a castle, and then by a country house. Some finds are at Carlisle but there is nothing whatever to be seen on the site today.

8. Hinterland forts

Immediately south of Hadrian's Wall was a series of strongholds on an east-west road stretching from Corbridge to, at least, Carlisle and perhaps as far as the fort at Kirkbride about 30 miles (50km) west of Carlisle. The road, which actually runs south-west from Carlisle and not out to Kirkbride, is now known as the 'Stanegate', an old word made up 'Stane' meaning stone, and 'Gate' or 'Yate' meaning street. The road exploited the low-lying land of the valleys of the Tyne and Irthing. Whether road and forts constituted a frontier 'system' in any formal sense, or merely a series of garrisons connected by road for efficient transit of troops and communications is unknown. The arrangement seems to date from Trajan's reign (98–117) and may have been some sort of consolidation of northern Britain following the withdrawal from Scotland during the mid-80s; several of the forts seem to have been in existence since around then. A similar system of forward road and rearward forts was in operation on the German frontier. However, the known Stanegate forts concentrate in the central and western sectors – there is little trace of anything to the east of Corbridge. Not much can be seen of the Stanegate system now, apart from the forts and settlements at Corbridge and Vindolanda.

It is important to appreciate that the hinterland forts were not necessarily occupied at the same time. The Vindolanda forts of the writing tablets, for example, predate the fort at South Shields. Moreover, calling them forts does rather imply that these were exclusively military bases concerned with fighting in some sort of way. But the Roman army was also perhaps the most important industrial organization of the ancient world and a great deal of activity in its establishments was given over to production of goods, equipment, food, animal transport, and storage. Army manpower was also allocated to garrison, guarding, mining, policing, and other duties. The hinterland forts of Hadrian's Wall will have played an extremely important role in all these activities, and probably operated in quite different capacities at different times.

As with the outpost forts Corbridge, Vindolanda, and South Shields do not make a convenient itinerary in their own right. All are highly recommended visits. The order in which they are described here indicates no degree of

76   *The water tank and channels, and beyond the remains of the two third-century granaries at Corbridge. The column bases and steps into the eastern granary can be seen at upper centre left.*

priority. Corbridge and Vindolanda are easily visited as detours from the Wall or as individual tours from local centres like Hexham. South Shields is sufficiently remote to be way off any normal day-trip to the Wall but this should not (and does not) discourage its many visitors. It's perhaps best visited in association with a trip to the Wall fort at Wallsend over the river, or the monastery of the eighth-century historian and monk Bede at Jarrow.

CORBRIDGE (*Coria* or *Coriosopitum*)

★★*Visible remains*★★: *town and military base. English Heritage. Entrance fee. Open all year round (10.00–6.00 1 April–31 October; 10.00–4.00 in winter; closed 1.00–2.00 in winter). Tel: 01434–632349. Access south from the A69 heading west out of Newcastle or by a short detour from the B6318 on the line of the Wall 2.5 miles (4km) to the north at Port Gate, just west of the site of the fort at Haltonchesters. Access, signposted, from minor road leading west from Corbridge's centre. OS Ref. NY 982648 (Sheet 87 1:50 000 Series).*

Roman *Coria* or *Coriosopitum* lay to the west of the modern town on the north bank of the Tyne. The name is restored from the corrupt *Corstopitum*; its true form is unknown, and of uncertain meaning, but appears to be named *Coria* on a wooden tablet from Vindolanda. Like South Shields, Corbridge was a major military base to the rear of Hadrian's Wall. The exposed remains represent only a small part of the Roman settlement. The museum looks out across the footings of two ranges of buildings on either side of an exposed section of east-

77   *Mullion in the eastern granary at Corbridge. This allowed air to circulate under the floor and thus prevent grain from becoming damp.*

west street, part of the original Stanegate trans-province route.

The first fort at Corbridge lay around 0.6 mile (1km) west at Red House and was discovered when the modern A69 was built over it. Dating to the late 70s, it was probably built by Agricola during his campaign deep into northern Britain. A decade later the garrison moved to a new turf fort on the present site. It lasted barely more than ten years itself before being burnt to the ground. There followed a complicated series of forts, and it was not until the end of the 130s that a stone fort was built. Thereafter the history of the site becomes even more complicated thanks to a succession of different plans and buildings. This is no more evident than in the height of the Stanegate Road in the middle of the site compared to exposed lower levels of buildings on either side. By the mid-second century Corbridge ceased to serve as a 'conventional' fort, if indeed it had ever been as simple as that, and within fifty years or so military administrative structures like the headquarters building had been done away with. Corbridge might have become a civilian settlement, possibly with official local-government status, but nothing is known for certain other than that it retained military connections.

The granaries and 'storehouse'
Passing outside the museum look out across the first two buildings to the north (left) of the Stanegate. These were granaries. Both retain the lower courses of

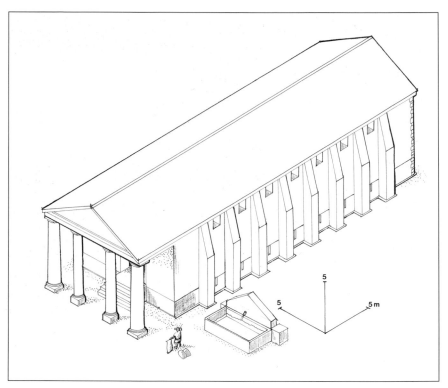

78   *Isometric reconstruction of the east granary at Corbridge. Third century.*

their massive walls and buttresses (**76**). Within, some of the flooring is still in place overlying channels which allowed air to circulate through the mullioned windows at waist-height. One of these is still in the east wall of the eastern granary (**77**). Note the column bases in front of the granaries, and how they abut the higher road, emphasizing the change in ground level during Roman times. They probably supported projecting porticoes providing covered access to the granaries (**78**).

Immediately to the east water was fed in down an aqueduct channel from higher ground to the north. It poured out of a fountain into a water tank which is still partly intact. The large dips in the wall panels were probably caused by washing clothes, and the sharpening of tools, knives, and other armaments. On either side overflows were carried away in open sluices for dispersal around the site.

The date of the granaries is uncertain but they were probably begun in the late second century, being abandoned some time during their construction and were not completed until the early third century. Just beyond them are the remains of an incomplete large courtyard building which remained unfinished. Scattered blocks suggest it was left as it was (**79**). It may have been a storehouse, or alternatively been intended for administration.

79   *Unfinished masonry forming part of a projected late second-century building, perhaps a store, at Corbridge. Some of the rough-hewn blocks have been fitted into place while others await installation.*

The Severan base

Corbridge was reorganized in the early third century, perhaps associated with Septimius Severus' Caledonian campaign. Like South Shields, Corbridge was almost certainly utilized as a store base. The granaries were completed, and to the south of the Stanegate the ground was divided up into walled compounds containing buildings for military accommodation, administration, and manufacturing. Their enclosure walls carefully skirted around existing roadside temples, for example opposite the granaries. Behind these temples, in the south-west corner of the present-day site, are the remains of a possible headquarters building with an underground strongroom. The undulations in wall footings hereabouts are attributed to natural settling, not buried ditches from earlier forts.

The various temples were eventually pulled down and Corbridge apparently became an industrial centre for the remainder of the Roman period. Post-Roman settlement drifted to the east and the old site was robbed for stones. Much of Hexham Abbey 3 miles (4.8km) from here was built out of Roman masonry, including many inscriptions and tombstones, which are almost certainly from Corbridge. One tombstone at the Abbey of a standard-bearer of the *Ala Petriana* called Flavinus probably belongs to the earliest phase of Corbridge's history; it also shows that the unit which eventually became stationed at Stanwix on the Wall once was here (a cast is on show at Corbridge). An inscription in the Abbey crypt records the building of a granary between

80   Impression taken from the Corbridge pottery mould depicting the Celtic warrior god Taranis. The spoked wheel symbolized the sun and its rays and is a familiar feature of Romano-Celtic religious iconography.

198–209, perhaps one of those on display at Corbridge (Source 18). Within modern Corbridge itself the Saxon St Andrew's church has a west porch, nave walls, and tower arch built of Roman masonry.

Museum

In here are various stone reliefs including a monumental inscription erected by a vexillation of the VI Legion under the governorship of Sextus Calpurnius Agricola in about 163 (Sources 12, 13, and 25). It probably records rebuilding work associated with the reoccupation of Hadrian's Wall early in the reign of Marcus Aurelius. Its top line once read *Soli Invicto*, 'to the Unconquered Sun' but was subsequently erased probably in connection with the *damnatio memoriae* of Commodus in 193, or Elagabalus (218–22) who favoured the Sun-God with such fanatical zeal that he and his mother were murdered in 222. Under such circumstances names, or anything else to do with individuals whose memory was to be damned, were scratched out of inscriptions. There are also numerous other reliefs and carvings of religious association, many of which must once have come from the temples here.

One of the most unusual small finds is a pottery mould which was used to create clay plaques depicting a Romano-Celtic warrior god (**80**). These plaques were probably affixed to pottery vessels. Warrior-gods of this type were common in Roman Britain and especially in military areas. The god is depicted here with a wheel, a common motif in Romano-Celtic religion. The spokes and wheel hub probably provided a convenient representation of the sun and its rays.

VINDOLANDA (Chesterholm)

★★Visible remains★★: fort, vicus, reconstructed stone Wall and Turf Wall (Map 5). Museum. Vindolanda Trust. Entrance fee (10% discount for English Heritage members). Site open daily from mid-February to mid-November with seasonal closing times from 4.00–6.30. Tel: 01434–344277. Access from Twice Brewed crossroads on the B6318 2.6 miles (4km) west of Housesteads car-park. Vindolanda is signposted to the left (south). Pass the picnic park on the right and carry on for about 0.5 mile (0.8km) to a left turn signposted to Vindolanda which lies 1 mile (1.6km) east of here. OS Ref. NY 770664 (Sheet 87 1:50 000 Series; Sheet 546 1:25 000 Series).

Vindolanda was not a Wall fort but the site has been developed as a monument to the whole way of life on the frontier. It is one of the most remarkable of all the sites in the area. The modern name is Chesterholm but the Roman name of *Vindolanda* ('bright heath' – the location is certainly well-lit) has always been applied to the modern site, both in books and on signposts.

The approach road to the car-park follows the course of the Stanegate which ran on east to the probable fort site at Newbrough, and the base at Corbridge. Not much of the Stanegate can be followed on a modern road, and this is the only stretch which runs up to a visible Roman fort. Watch out for a Roman milestone (uninscribed) in its original position on the north side of the road, a very unusual sight in Britain.

On the footpath from the car-park a straggle of Roman buildings can be seen on either side of a winding road which leads to the west gate of the stone fort. These are the remains of the *vicus*, the only one visible on the whole Wall area, apart from a few scattered footings outside Housesteads. The visible military remains are principally those of the fourth-century fort but the site had a much longer history. To the south of the settlement, and further down the slope, are reconstructed stretches of Hadrian's Wall in turf and stone. These were erected here for experimental and display purposes only: Vindolanda was not a Wall fort though some books contribute to the impression that it was.

Vindolanda began life in the first century like Corbridge as a large timber and earth fort with a complicated history stretching over forty or more years from about the year 80 – at least five consecutive forts seem to have been built on the site during that period. Each new fort was built on top of the only partly-demolished remains of its predecessor, explaining the great depth of the earliest levels more than 20ft (6m) under later Roman debris. It is from these levels that the remarkable series of writing tablets and other perishable goods like leather shoes and wooden tools have been recovered from waterlogged deposits.

The fifth timber fort was demolished around the time that the Wall was built, being replaced during the mid-second century by a 3.5 acre (1.4ha) stone fort on a different alignment. Hadrian's visit to Britain seems to have coincided with an extravagantly-appointed and substantial timber courtyard building erected nearby. With more than 50 rooms and painted wall-plaster it is entirely out of context with more ordinary military buildings. The excavated section lies just outside the west gate of the stone fort and appears to continue underneath the fort. So, the building was clearly not very long-lived. Apparently constructed between 120–30, it was perhaps built for Hadrian, the provincial governor, Aulus Platorius Nepos, or an unknown official in charge of Wall building, as a headquarters. This is only speculation and its full extent or purpose will probably never be known.

The new stone fort was completely rebuilt in the early third century; the visible remains belong to this phase and subsequent repairs and rebuilding on into the fourth century. Whether the *vicus* lasted as long as the fort is not entirely certain. The recovery of datable finds suggests it was given up by the end of the fourth century or not much later.

The vicus

Head down through the main street of the *vicus* towards the fort. The alignment of the road and the asymmetrical rectangular buildings emphasise the differences between the regimented lay-out of a Roman fort and more spontaneous civilian development. The first substantial building on the south side of the vicus 'high street' was either a *mansio* or a military officer's house. A *mansio* was a kind of official inn and often served as the stimulus to the development of minor settlements. In the military zone a *mansio* would have been used by government and military officials travelling along the frontier or en route to the north. The possible Vindolanda example was built on an eccentric plan and had three wings wedged round a narrow courtyard which fronted the street.

The most interesting building in the *vicus* today is the bath-house in the northern part. Its well-preserved walls are more than 6.5ft (2m) in height. This was the fort bath-house and, like those at Chesters, Housesteads, and elsewhere, it lay outside the fort walls. It was built during the mid-second century, perhaps by the VI Legion because its stamped bricks were found in a stoke-hole arch.

As built the bath-house consisted of six main chambers in two north-south, off-set, rows. These formed the main bath-suite of cold, warm, and hot rooms. An apse in the western half was the hot plunge bath. This was soon augmented by adding a changing room and entrance to the east, with latrine attached, and an expanded boiler room to the north-west beyond the apse. When excavated the structure had to be cleared of substantial deposits of hardened soot, and then consolidated to make good the damage caused by the heat under the floors.

81   Altar from Vindolanda (now at Chesters) dedicated to Jupiter (Iuppiter Optimus Maximus) by Quintus Petronius Urbicus of the Fourth Cohort of Gauls. Third century(?).

The various other structures in the *vicus* are difficult to interpret from what are fairly unsophisticated ground plans but are likely to have been shops and houses. It would have been populated by the families, legitimate or otherwise, of the fort's personnel and perhaps retired soldiers eking out a living.

The fort

The stone fort was occupied in the third and fourth century by the Fourth Cohort of Gauls (**81**). The road from the *vicus* heads straight up to the fort's west gate. It was of single-portal type with a pair of guard towers, as was the north gate. The restoration by the Gauls of one of these gates 'with towers' was recorded on a fragmentary inscription, now lost, dating to 222–35. Anyone coming here from Housesteads will notice that these gates are very small by comparison. The east and south gates are even smaller, and had no guard towers. Within the ramparts only the headquarters building is visible today (**82**), though the adjacent commanding officer's house was re-excavated in 1997 (Source 1a).

The headquarters building was of conventional form, with an entrance through a courtyard leading into the main cross-hall, but the courtyard was very small. In the hall note the tribunal to the west from where the unit's

82   *The headquarters building at Vindolanda looking south-east.*

senior officers would have addressed an assembly of troops. The rear range of rooms is distinguished by the survival of some of the stone screens (**83**). These closed off the chambers and their contents in a similar way to the low brass or stone screens which mark chapels in cathedrals or large churches. The central chamber was reached through a small room off the hall with benches. Beyond was the chapel of the unit's standards.

Museum

The museum lies east of the fort down a path, and is without doubt the most interesting one on the Wall at the present time, thanks largely to the environmental conditions in areas of the site. As a result wooden writing tablets, wooden tools, leather, and textile artefacts survive intact but decay rapidly on exposure to the air.

Much of the history of Vindolanda's excavation has been the story of the discovery of these finds, followed by their urgent consolidation and preservation. Many are on display in the museum here and it's worth remembering that all these items, such as wooden bowls and tools, would have existed everywhere else in the Roman world. It is merely the process of decay that creates the false impression that Roman artefacts were mainly pottery, stone, and bronze. Thousands of leather shoes have been recovered from the same levels as the writing tablets and some may even have belonged to the individuals named in the correspondence. The finds also include wooden hair combs, an axle from a cart, carpentry tools and three-legged stools. The

83   Stone screen in the Vindolanda headquarters building.

museum also contains the inscribed slab found in 1997 which may refer to a northern war around the time that Hadrian's Wall was conceived and begun (Source 1).

The most important finds are the wooden writing tablets (now at the British Museum in London) which record much of the comings and goings of the individuals who lived and worked here at the end of the first century. More than a thousand have been recovered, but most are too damaged to be legible. Of those that are, some record straightforward social arrangements while others go into details of problems with pre-Hadrianic garrisoning and supplies at Vindolanda. One, for instance, announces that roads in the area are so wretched that a delayed consignment of hides should be freighted in on the backs of mules instead. Some idea of the Romans' feelings about local hostility comes from a tablet which describes the Britons use of disorderly and guerrilla-type cavalry tactics. The word used for the Britons here is *Brittunculi*, a derogatory form which suggests they were regarded as relentlessly irritating and disruptive, but doesn't specify whether they were enemies or useless local recruits. Unfortunately these finds all predate the Wall and while giving us an impression of Roman life in the frontier zone what they don't provide is specific information about garrisoning and administering the Wall.

If a visit to Vindolanda has been a detour from the Wall return to the B6318 by the same route. On the B6318 head north straight over Twice Brewed cross-roads for Steel Rigg car-park, or turn left and head west for Cawfields milecastle.

SOUTH SHIELDS (*Arbeia*)

★★*Visible remains*★★: *fort lay-out, with rebuilt west gate. Under local authority guardianship. Free. Open all year round (closed Mondays and Sundays, except Sunday afternoon opening from 2.00–5.00 in summer). Tel: 0191–454–4093. Access by road is via the A185/A194 from Gateshead (passing the church and monastery site of Bede at Jarrow). Approaching South Shields up the A194, watch out for a roundabout exit to the B1303 (Station Road, becoming River Drive) which skirts round the north of South Shields by the Tyne and turn right (south) down Baring Street. The fort is on your left. However, South Shields is a confusing place for the stranger and an A–Z guide is thoroughly recommended because the fort is poorly signposted. Access by Metro (South Shields Station) involves a 15–20 minute walk: head east down King Street and carry on into Ocean Road, take the first left turn after the roundabout (Baring Street) and walk north for half a mile (0.8km) to the museum. A–Z map Site p. 35 E5, Metro p. 51 1E. OS Ref. NZ 365679 (Sheet 88 1:50 000 Series).*

The fort at South Shields (*Arbeia*, meaning unknown – perhaps derived from a name for the river or estuary in the vicinity, or even connected with the home of its fourth-century garrison in *Arabia*) has suffered a similar fate to Wallsend across the Tyne to the west. The opportunity for substantial excavation has not been missed here either; now Wallsend and South Shields stand alongside one another as the two of the best-known forts in the whole Wall area. A visit to South Shields is a detour from everywhere else on the northern frontier. It lies far to the east of all the others and is a complicated place to drive to, even from Newcastle. It is, however, relatively easily reached by public transport.

The site overlooks Tynemouth to the east and the river to the west and north and was appropriately garrisoned in the fourth century by a unit of 'Tigris Boatmen'. The first stone fort was existence by the 160s. The reason for a fort here is fairly obvious. Even the extension of the Wall to Wallsend left more than 4 miles (6.5 km) of the Tyne estuary apparently unsupervised. Various inscribed stones indicate that the VI Legion was responsible for building the fort. The First Ala of Asturians, a cavalry unit, is mentioned on the undated tombstone of the freedman Victor and may have been the garrison. It is possible that there had been an even earlier fort here – some late first-century finds make it a credible theory, but no definitive early military fort structures apart from a parade ground have been found.

In the early third century South Shields was transformed into a non-standard fort (**84**). The south rampart was demolished and a new one built beyond to enlarge the fort by more than a quarter to 5.2 acres (2.1ha). This work is also associated with the VI Legion (a stone marking the work of its third cohort has recently been found by the south-east corner of the extension). Instead of the normal barracks surrounding the central administrative block, almost the entire original fort area was covered by 22 granaries. Even the headquarters building was cleared away to make room. The garrison was moved into barracks in the extension, along with a new, smaller

84   Plan of the fort at South Shields. 1 Entrance to fort from museum. 2 Reconstructed west gate. 3 North gate. 4 Headquarters building. 5 Early fort south-east corner protruding from extended rampart. 6 Latrine. 7 Early parade ground. 8 Fourth-century barracks. 9 Fourth-century commanding officer's house. (Based on various published plans and used by permssion of Paul Bidwell, Principal Keeper, South Shields Roman Fort.)

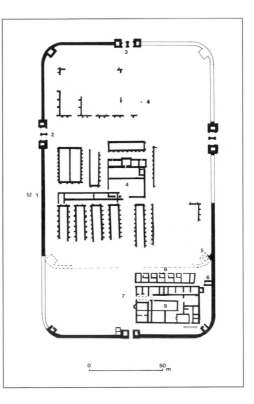

headquarters building.

South Shields had thus been transformed into a fortified store base, perhaps associated with Septimius Severus' Scottish campaign. The Fifth Cohort of Gauls is mentioned on lead seals (probably from grain sacks), and on an inscription of 222 recording an aqueduct here (Source 18). The unit was also at the Severan fort of Cramond in Scotland at an unspecified date, though of course it may have been split between the two forts. Some of the seals bear images of Severus and his two sons, and co-rulers, Caracalla and Geta. An altar here was dedicated during their joint rule after their father's death in 211.

However, the building of granaries here seems to have gone on right up to about the year 230; so the fort may also have been devised as a long-term stores base for the Wall. This store fort subsequently burnt down, around the year 300. During the fourth century it was repaired for a more conventional role, with barracks being built amongst, and even out of, the granaries and a new headquarters building erected on the site of the long-demolished first one.

The fort had a civilian settlement outside its walls. Some of the tombstones on display in the museum testify to its cosmopolitan population. Regina was a member of the Catuvellauni, a tribe whose region was in south-east Britain near *Verulamium* (St Albans). She had been a slave but was freed by her master Barates, a Syrian from Palmyra, who commissioned her elaborate tombstone when she died at the age of 30 (**85**). Unfortunately, her face has been destroyed

141

but she is depicted in a wicker chair, apparently engaged in mending clothes. It's a touching domestic portrayal of a woman who was clearly mourned. So too was the 20-year-old freedman Victor from the province of Mauretania in north-west Africa, 'devotedly conducted' to his grave by his former master Numerianus, a trooper in the First Ala of Asturians, and thought by some to be evidence of a homosexual relationship. Although different in detail both tombstones resemble one another in presenting their subjects in architectural frames, and it has been suggested that they were carved by the same sculptor. The style resembles the architecture of the Eastern Empire, so perhaps the sculptor was from the East. Neither tombstone can be dated but parallels from Syria suggest the mid-second century or later.

The many other finds on display in the museum include some of the jewellery and cameos found here, as well as items made of jet. Waste jet indicates there was a local industry manufacturing goods for the local market and also for sale across the North Sea in Gaul and Germany.

Within the fort turn left. No-one can fail to be struck by the imposing west gate, a replica of which was built in 1986 (**86**). It's best seen from outside the site and gives a superb idea of the original appearance of a massive twin-portalled Roman military gateway. Little is certain in Romano-British archaeology and this is no less true of the gate's restored upper-storey and

86   *The reconstructed west gate at South Shields looking from outside the fort. The gate was probably erected originally in the middle of the second century, and has now been rebuilt on the Roman foundations and plan. The form is probably roughly right but the height is uncertain as clearly the existence of a first storey must remain speculative.*

roofing. Nevertheless, the original gate is unlikely to have differed much, and would certainly have been of similar scale as the reconstruction is built on the original foundations and based on architectural fragments recovered such as arched window heads. The reconstruction involved a dozen workers for around a year, a sobering thought considering this is only one gate of four on a fort which is itself only one of dozens in a region which had never seen building like this before.

Various items are displayed within the replica gate, such as a model of the fort undergoing transformation into a supply base, and photographs of the modern reconstruction work. It's also a useful place to look over the fort and see how it commanded excellent views across the river to the north.

The *via principalis* led from the west gate across to the east gate. On either side are now the footings of some of the numerous granaries. A large area of the fort is now exposed. In the middle are the remains of the final-phase headquarters building surrounded by the footings of several of the granaries. To the left are the remains of the north gate, and these give an impression of how the west gate appeared before modern rebuilding began.

The south-eastern area of South Shields fort is in many ways the most interesting. This was part of the extension to the second-century fort, built at the beginning of the third century to accommodate the supply-base troops. The old south-east corner of the original fort can be spotted protruding from the eastern wall. It escaped demolition by being incorporated into the new

143

earthen rampart stacked up behind the fort wall. Just beyond it is the latrine building, not as well-preserved as the example at Housesteads but its underfloor channels to carry waste away are still visible.

Excavations in the fort extension have shown a remarkable sequence which began with an Iron-Age roundhouse. This had burnt down in the third-century BC, long before the Romans arrived. On its site a fort parade ground was laid, then just outside the southern rampart of the second-century fort. It may have belonged to an even earlier, but unlocated, timber fort. When the stone fort was enlarged into a store base this area was used for barracks, remaining that way until the fire of c.300. A new parade ground was laid out to the north-east of the fort, and was identified under modern buildings a number of years ago.

The south-east part of the fort was used for the biggest structure on the site, a large courtyard house which may have been the fourth-century commanding officer's home. It has turned out to be an unusual discovery for this part of the world at this date. The house was constructed in traditional classical form with an entrance into a colonnaded hall, with rooms ranged around an internal garden of the type anyone who has visited Pompeii, in Italy, will be familiar with. The rooms included an internal bath-suite and two dining rooms *(triclinia)*, one heated and one unheated. It was probably built to provide the commanding officer with accommodation he was accustomed to.

There is some evidence that *Arbeia* remained in use into the post-Roman period; it's very unlikely that such a prominent, and fortified, place could have served no purpose. It may be the *Caer Urfa*, reported by the sixteenth-century antiquarian John Leland to be the birth-place of Oswin, King of Deira (a Northumbrian kingdom), who died in approximately 651. *Caer* means 'camp' or 'fort', and *Urfa* is believed to be a possible contraction of *Arbeia*.

★★★★★

There were many other forts of various dates in northern Britain to the south of the Wall. Roger Wilson's excellent *Guide to the Roman Remains in Britain* (third edition, Constable 1988, reprinted 1997) is the best source of detailed information on access and what to see at sites like Old Carlisle, Binchester, Piercebridge, and Ebchester.

Sources for Hadrian's Wall

The history of the Wall and the northern frontier is far from exact. There are few fixed points and thus no evading the fact that the accepted chronology not infrequently hangs or falls by an inferred word on a damaged inscription, if one even exists. This is not always apparent in histories of Roman Britain. So that readers may decide for themselves the main evidence is summarized here with some examples provided in full. They should prove of value to those interested in pursuing the evidence for Wall history, and also to archaeologists and teachers. Latin sources are supplied in Latin and translation. Others are supplied in translation only. I have either paraphrased or translated the inscriptions. Abbreviations and references appear in the Bibliography.

Restored sections of inscriptions are indicated []. Letters intentionally omitted for the sake of abbreviation are here indicated () where the sense is difficult. Composite characters, where two or more letters are combined into a single symbol, have been invariably expanded. Where words are split between lines a hyphen (-) indicates thus; these do not appear on the inscriptions. Supplementary information is supplied in the form of brief details of additional inscriptions where they confirm, complicate, or augment the source cited. Full details of inscriptions not given here in full appear mostly in *RIB* and *Lactor* no.4 (see Bibliography: Inscriptions and other sources).

1. Hadrian's frontier policy AD 117, and 122

a. ... *Britanni teneri sub Romana dicione not poterant ...*
'The Britons were not able to be restrained under Roman control.' This reference to the beginning of Hadrian's reign in 117 suggests that there was war in Britain. That losses had been heavy in Britain, and Judaea, under Hadrian was alluded to by Marcus Cornelius Fronto in an extant letter to the Emperor Lucius Verus written c.162 (Fronto: see the Loeb edition, vol.ii, pp.22/23).

A 1997 find of a memorial slab at Vindolanda reused in the late commandant's house records the death of a centurion commanding a unit of Tungrians in a northern war in Britain early in the second century, dated on style and content. The tombstone of Titus Pontius Sabinus from Ferentini in Italy records his participation in a British expedition (*expeditione Brittannica*), involving detachments of the VII *Gemina*, VIII *Augusta*, and XXII *Primigenia*, around this time (Lactor no.4, source 47). The latter two legions supplied detachments under Antoninus Pius too (Source 9, below).

b. ... *Britanniam petiit, in qua multa correxit murumque per octoginta milia passuum primus duxit, qui barbaros Romanosque divideret.*
After his time in Germany Hadrian 'set out for Britain where he reformed many things, and, the first [to do so], erected a wall over a length of eighty miles, which was to force apart the Romans and barbarians.'

c. *Per ea tempora et alias frequenter in plurimis locis, in quibus barbari non fluminibus sed limitibus dividuntur, stipitibus magnis in modum muralis saepis funditus iactis atque conexis barbaros separavit.*
(*SHA. Hadrian.* v.2, xi.2, and xii.6.)
'Throughout this time and often others in many places, in which they are restrained not by rivers but by artificial frontiers, [Hadrian] kept the barbarians out with tall stakes stuck deep into the

earth and lashed together in the form of a palisade.'

The date of 122 for the Wall in Britain is inferred from the sequence of Hadrian's travels detailed by his biographer, and the association of his name with that of the governor Aulus Platorius Nepos on primary inscriptions from the Wall (see 2–4 below). It would be more accurate to say that a range of 120–22 for commencing building is possible.

2. Milecastle 38(?). Hadrianic dedicatory inscription (3). c.122–4+
IMP CAES TRAIAN
HADRIANI AVG
LEG II AVG
A PLATORIO NEPOTE LEG PR [PR]   (*RIB* 1638)
'The Second Legion Augusta (built this milecastle) under the governor Aulus Platorius Nepos (in honour of) of the Emperor Caesar Trajan Hadrian Augustus.'

Found near milecastle 38 (Hotbank), attributing a structure to Hadrian between 117–28, and the governorship of the propraetorian legate Aulus Platorius Nepos (c.122–4+). Other examples of similar, but fragmentary, inscriptions in stone survive from nearby (*RIB* 1637), from milecastles 37 and 42 (*RIB* 1634, 1666). Another, from west of Birdoswald, but of wood (*RIB* 1935, legion uncertain), was found at the Turf Wall milecastle 50. Two diplomas confirm that Nepos began his governorship in 122 and was still the incumbent in 124 (see Source 25).

3. Benwell. Hadrianic dedicatory inscription. c.122–4+
IMP CAES TRAIANO
HADRI[AN]• **AVG**
A•PLATORIO N[EPOTE L]**EG AVG PR P**
VEXILLATO C[LASSIS] **BRITAN**   (*RIB* 1340)
'A vexillation of the British Fleet (built this) under the governor Aulus Platorius Nepos for the Emperor Caesar Trajan Hadrian Augustus.'

From a fort granary, recording that under Nepos a detachment of the Roman Fleet in Britain erected the building. Two centurial stones from further west name the Fleet for having built part of the curtain too (*RIB* 1944, 1945).

4. Haltonchesters. Hadrianic dedicatory inscription. c.122–4+
IMP CAES T[RAIAN HADRIANO]
AVG LEG•VI•V[ICTRIX]
A PLATORIO N[EPOTE]
LEG AVG•PR [PR]   (*RIB* 1427)
'The Sixth Legion Victrix (built this) under the governor Aulus Platorius Nepos for the Emperor Caesar Trajan Hadrian Augustus.'

Found outside the west gate, and easily restored to show that it was dedicated by the VI Legion during the reign of Hadrian and the governorship of Nepos. The Legion appears to have arrived in Britain with Hadrian.

5. Greatchesters. Hadrianic dedicatory inscription. c.128?–38
IMP CAES TRAI(A)**N HAD**[RI]**A-**
NO AVG•P[ATER]•**P**[ATRIAE]   (*RIB* 1736)
'To the Emperor Caesar Trajan Hadrian Augustus, Father of the Country.'

From outside the east gate. Hadrian became *Pater Patriae* in 128. This inscription has been taken to show that Greatchesters belongs to the latter part of his reign. Julian Bennett has noted, however, that the title occasionally appears on inscriptions of earlier date, for example a milestone from near Leicester of 119–20 (*RIB* 2244, see *Britannia* xv, 1984, 234–5). The inscription is oddly composed with only a brief text inscribed into the lower half of an otherwise blank ansate panel (**87**). R.P. Wright's suggestion that this was to make it more easily read by someone looking up at the gate is very unlikely because it was never done anywhere else. Perhaps the panel was installed as a blank, and later carved *in situ* by someone who did not know exactly when and by whom the fort had been built, and who was unable to reach properly. The sagging of the end of the first line makes this plausible. The inscription is thus not certain evidence for Greatchesters' late Hadrianic date.

6. Later Hadrianic governors. c.126–38

Aulus Platorius Nepos was succeeded by Trebius Germanus. He is mentioned only on a single diploma, which surfaced in 1997, naming him as governor of Britain on 20 August 127. The diploma was presented to a soldier of Dacian origin, called Itaxa, in the Second Cohort of Lingones. Germanus has yet to be testified for certain on any building inscription from Britain, and his absence (for the moment) suggests that much of the primary construction on the Wall was very advanced by c.126. Sextus Julius Verus was governor between c.130 and 134 (*RIB* 739 from Bowes, but incomplete and long lost). *RIB* 1550 from Carrawburgh is reputed to name Verus, thus 'proving' the fort's late Hadrianic date but in fact only parts of two letters of a governor's(?) name survive (and none of the emperor's, or his, titles) so it is of dubious value. Publius Mummius Sisenna is named as governor on 14 April 135, but his full name is only known from a career inscription (Birley 1979, 173). Apart from Nepos none is thus unequivocally associated with building on the Wall.

7. Hadrianic occupation at Carvoran. 136–8

• FORTVNAE • AVG •
• PRO • SALVTE • L • AELI
• CAESARIS • EX • VISV
• I • FLA • SECVNDVS •
PRAEF • COH • I • HAM-
IORVM • SAGITTAR
• V • S • L • M •   (*RIB* 1778)

'To Augustan Fortune for the health of Lucius Aelius Caesar, Titus Flavius Secundus, prefect of the First Cohort of Hamian Archers, willingly and deservedly fulfilled his vow, because of a vision.'

Dedicated to Lucius Aelius Caesar during his brief period (136–8) as Hadrian's heir. Inscriptions from the fort (Source 8) name Secundus as prefect responsible for stone ramparts. The altar provides fixed dates for part of Secundus' term and therefore the building though he may obviously have been there for longer. The First Cohort of Hamians was at Bar Hill on the Antonine Wall (e.g. *RIB* 2167, 2172) before returning to Carvoran by 163–6, recorded on an inscription (*RIB* 1792) mentioning the governor Calpurnius Agricola, himself dated to the reign of Marcus Aurelius (Source 12).

8. Hadrianic building at Carvoran. 136–8

SILVANI •
VALLAVIT •
P • CXII • SVB
FLA • SECVNDO
[PRA]EF •   (*RIB* 1820)

'Silvanus' century built 112 feet of rampart under command of the prefect Flavius Secundus.'
    See Source 7.

9. The Antonine Wall. 138–41

Per legatos suos plurima bella gessit. Nam et Britannos per Lollium Urbicum vicit legatum alio muro caespiticio summotis barbaris ducto … .
(*SHA. Antoninus Pius*, v.4).

'Through his legates [Antoninus Pius] waged many wars. For example through the legate Lollius Urbicus he defeated the Britons, and built another wall, of turf, having driven back the barbarians… .'

An inscription from High Rochester names Lollius Urbicus as governor (*RIB* 1276) showing that it was reoccupied about now. Another (*RIB* 2110), from Birrens but dated to 158 by Pius' titles

87   *Inscription from Greatchesters. See Source 5. Width 1.12m. Now at Chesters.*

for that year, shows occupation in the reign of Antoninus Pius by the Second Cohort of, what can be probably restored as, Tungrians. A recently-discovered inscription from Birrens, undated but of Antonine style, names two legions from the Rhine here: VIII *Augusta* and XXII *Primigenia*. Perhaps Lollius Urbicus brought detachments of these legions with him to help with building work on the northern frontier (*Britannia* xxiii, 1992, 318; see also Source 1a above and *RIB* 2216).

10. War in Britain(?) under Pius. 138–61

'Antoninus ... took away much of the Brigantian land in Britain because they had set out on an armed invasion of the area called Genounia, which was under Roman control.' Pausanias, *Description of Greece* (xliii.3–4).

Genounia is unknown in Britain. However, there was another tribe called the Brigantes in the province of Raetia (equivalent roughly to Switzerland) and their neighbours happen to have been called the Genauni. Pausanias was probably confused by this and the reference thus probably does not refer to Britain.

11. Reinforcements at Newcastle under Antoninus Pius. c.155–9

```
IMP•ANTONI-
NO•AVG•PIO•P
PAT•VEXILATIO
LEG•II•AVG•ET•LEG
•VI•VIC•ET•LEG•
•XX•VV•CON(T)R(I)-
BVTI•EX•GER•DV-
OBVS•SVB•IVLIO•VE-
RO•LEG•AVG•PR•P•                    (RIB 1322)
```

Despite the state of preservation this inscription's meaning is far from certain. It may record that reinforcements for the II, VI, and XX Legions arrived from the two German armies in around 158; or, it may record that reinforcements from these legions were sent to Germany; or, it may commemorate the return of detachments from the legions which had been sent temporarily to

Germany. The approximate year of 158 comes from an inscription at Birrens naming Julius Verus as governor, dated precisely to between December 157 and December 158 (*RIB* 2110). The VI Legion was engaged on repairing the Wall at Heddon by 158, recorded by a centurial stone with an unusually specific record of the date (*RIB* 1389). Apart from the problems with meaning the carving is an exercise in caution in relying on modern reconstructions of damaged inscriptions; here the mason has miscalculated at the end of the fourth line, failing to leave room for 'LEG'. In consequence he has combined 'L' and 'E' and crammed in a diminutive 'G'. It's unlikely that this would be thought possible had this part of the block been found damaged (**17**).

12. Wars under Marcus Aurelius. 163
Imminebat etiam Britannicum bellum ... . Et adversus Britannos quidem Calpurnius Agricola missus est ... .
(*SHA. Marcus Aurelius* viii.7–8.)
'Besides, a British war was threatening ... . And in fact Calpurnius Agricola was sent against the Britons... .'

13. Reoccupation at Carvoran. c.163–6
DEAE SVRI-
AE SVB CALP-
VRNIO AG[R-
ICOL[A LE]**G AV**[G]
PR PR LIC[IN]**IVS**
[C]**LEM**[ENS PRAEF
C]**OH I HA**[MIOR]   (*RIB* 1792)
'To the Syrian Goddess, Licinius Clemens, prefect of the First Cohort of Hamians, set this up under the emperor's pro-praetorian legate Calpurnius Agricola.'

   Calpurnius Agricola's approximate dates as governor come from Source 12 (above) and an inscription from Corbridge which has been heavily restored to give the titles of Marcus Aurelius and Lucius Verus for the year 163 (*RIB* 1149). It is, however, plain from that restoration that the inscription could belong to anywhere between 163–6 and possibly earlier or even slightly later as none of the year-specific titles survives in full.

14. Reoccupation at Stanwix. 167
DEDIC[ATA]
IMP VERO [III ET]
VMIDIO [QUADRATO
COS...]   (*RIB* 2026)
'Dedicated during the year of the consulships of the Emperor Lucius Verus (for this third time) and Umidius Quadratus.'

   Found to the west of the fort. The joint consulship of Lucius Verus (joint emperor with Aurelius, 161–9) and Umidius Quadratus occurred in the year 167, thus providing a rare instance of a fixed year on the Wall following the abandonment of the Antonine Wall.

15. The war under Commodus. 184
'However, the most important war was in Britain. For the tribes in the island crossed the Wall which divided them from the Roman soldiers and did a huge amount of damage, even taking out a legate with his troops. In consequence Commodus grew worried and despatched Ulpius Marcellus against the tribes ... he inflicted serious defeats on the British barbarians.'
Cassius Dio, lxxiii.8.1–2

16. An aqueduct at Chesters. c.177/8–184
AQVA•ADDVCTA
ALAE•II•ASTVR•
SVB•VLP•MARCELLO
LEG•AVG•PR PR   (*RIB* 1463)

This records the 'bringing of water' by the Second Ala of Asturians during the governorship of Ulpius Marcellus. His dates come from Cassius Dio (Source 15), and a diploma dated 23 March 178 naming him as governor (see R.S.O. Tomlin in Collingwood and Wright, 1995, p. 783 for *RIB* 1329). He thus served under Marcus Aurelius (161–80), and Commodus (180–96), and during their period of joint rule (177–80) explaining an inscription from Benwell where he is named as serving under joint emperors (*RIB* 1329). However, prior to the discovery of the diploma it was thought impossible that one man could have remained in position so long and that therefore Cassius Dio's Marcellus, and the Marcellus of the inscriptions were two different men; a second Marcellus was thus postulated, and assigned to 211–12 in the joint reign of Caracalla and Geta. The residence of the Asturians and the building of the aqueduct were thus also assigned to that period. This is now discounted though confirming the late second-century garrison at Chesters remains complicated by a single undated stone from the fort bearing the name of a different unit, the First Cohort of Dalmatians (Birley 1961, 174).

17. Lucius Junius Victorinus and his exploits. c.150–80

L IVNIVS VIC-
TORINVS FL
CAELIANVS LEG
AVG LEG VI VIC
PF OB RES TRANS
VALLVM PRO-
SPERE GESTAS   (*RIB* 2034)

'Lucius Junius Victorinus Flavius Caelianus, imperial legate of the VI Legion *Victrix Pia Fidelis*, (erected this) on account of successful exploits across the wall.'

Found at Kirksteads, about 1.25 miles (2 km) south of the Wall at Kirkandrews upon Eden to the west of Carlisle. Dating is only approximate.

18. A granary built at Birdoswald. 205–8

IMPP C^ESS•L•
SEPT SEVERO PIO
PERT ET M AVR A[NT]O-
NINO ^VG [ET P SEP
GETAE NOB CAES] HOR-
REVM FECER COH I ^EL
DAC ET I T(H)RACVM C R SVB
^LFENO SENECIONE COS
PER ^VREL IVLIANVM TR   (*RIB* 1909)

'For the Emperor-Caesars Lucius Septimius Severus Pius Pertinax and Marcus Aurelius Antoninus [Caracalla], and Publius Septimius Geta, most noble Caesar [name erased after his brother Caracalla murdered him], the First Aelian Cohort of Dacians and the First Cohort of Thracians, Roman citizens, built the granary under the consular governor Alfenus Senecio through the tribune Aurelius Julianus.'

Found reused as a paving stone in a barrack block at Birdoswald. A considerable quantity of other building work of the early third century on the northern frontier is commemorated at Corbridge(?) on *RIB* 1151, now at Hexham Abbey, between 198–209 (granary), at Risingham by *RIB* 1234 for 205–7 (gate) and *RIB* 1235 for 213 (unspecified), at High Rochester by *RIB* 1279 (unspecified) for 216, 1280 and 1281 (*ballistaria* – see Source 21 below) for 220 and 225–35, *RIB* 1465 from Chesters (unspecified) for 221–2, by *RIB* 1060 (aqueduct) at South Shields for 222, by *RIB* 1738 (granary) from Greatchesters for 225, *RIB* 1553 from Carrawburgh (unspecified but naming the unit on the Mithraeum altars) for 237, and by *RIB* 1091 (baths) at Lanchester for 238–44.

19. Septimius Severus. 210–11

Britanniam, quod maximum eius imperii decus est, muro per transversam insulam ducto utrimque ad finem Oceani munivit. Unde etiam Britannici nomen accepit. (*SHA, Severus* xviii.2).

'Britain, which was the greatest glory of his reign, he fortified by building a wall right across the island to the shore of the Ocean on either side. From which also he accepted the name Britannicus.'

This version of events arose from Severus' extensive repair work on the Wall. The *Scriptores* is one of several fourth-century sources to have confused repair with original work, and it contributed to the belief that Severus had instigated the stone wall from the ground up. The statement is echoed in one of two incomplete inscriptions found at Jarrow, and thought to have come from a nearby Roman monument to the Wall; however, both inscriptions lack any specific dating information and may be either from a monument to Hadrian by Severus, or one contemporary with Hadrian (see Daniels, 1978, 54, or Collingwood and Wright, 1995, 349–51: *RIB* 1051a–b).

20. The east gate at Birdoswald. Early third century

SVB MODIO IV-
LIO LEG AVG PR•
PR COH•I•AEL•D(A)C•
CVI PRAEEST M
CL MENANDER
TRIB•   (*RIB* 1914)

'Under the Emperor's pro-praetorian legate Modius Julius, the first Aelian Cohort of Dacians, commanded by Marcus Claudius Menander (built this).'

Found by the east gate at Birdoswald. Modius' governorship is assigned to the year 219 on the dubious evidence of an imaginatively restored reading of a damaged and recut inscription from Netherby which may not even name him (*RIB* 980; see Collingwood and Wright, 1995, pp. 327, 777, and pl. xv). The style is, however, of the early third century. It will have been matched by a stone with the relevant emperor's titles.

21. Rebuilding at Birdoswald. 297–305

DDN]N•DIO[CLETIANO] ET
M[AX]IMIANO INVICTIS AVGG ET
CONSTANTIO ET MAXIMIANO
N•N•C•C•SVB VP•AVR•ARPAGIO PR
PRAETOR•QVOD ERAT HVMO COPERT
ET IN LABE CONL ET PRINC•ET BAL•R(E)ST
CVRANT•FL•MARTINO•CENT•PP•C... (*RIB* 1912)

'For the Lords Diocletian and Maximianus, the Invincible Augusti, and for Constantius and [Galerius] Maximianus, the most Noble Caesars, under his Perfection Aurelius Arpagius, governor, (the Cohort ... restored) the commandant's house which had fallen into ruin and was covered in earth, and the headquarters building and the bath-house(?), under the direction of Flavius Martinus, centurion in command ... .'

Found, as Source 18. A fragment of a contemporary and apparently similar inscription has survived from Housesteads (*RIB* 1613). The restoration of BAL as *balneum* (bath-house) has been disputed (see G.H. Donaldson in *Britannia* xxi, 1990, 207ff, and Tomlin's note to this inscription in *RIB* 1995, p. 782) and may be an abbreviation for *ballistarium*, a word of uncertain meaning and otherwise only attested at High Rochester (see Source 18).

22. Fourth- and fifth-century historical references

There are too many references to the later history of Roman Britain to be included here. Few are specific and range from the *Notitia Dignitatum* to rambling rants and passing mentions. The best source for these is Ireland, S., 1986 (see Bibliography).

23. The Wall in the eighth century. 731

'... to help these allies whom they had had to abandon, [the Romans] constructed a strong stone wall in a straight line from shore to shore, where Severus had built his earthwork, between the cities that had been founded as strongholds. This well-known and still conspicuous wall was built out of the public purse and private cash, with the Britons helping out. It is eight feet wide, and twelve high and ran directly from east to west, as anyone can see clearly to this day.'
(Bede. *History of the English Church and People*, I.xii.)

24. Principal Roman Emperors (all dates AD)

Claudius	41–54
Nero	54–68
Vespasian	69–79
Titus	79–81
Domitian	81–96
Nerva	96–8
Trajan	98–117
Hadrian	117–38 (with Lucius Aelius as heir 136–8)
Antoninus Pius	138–61 (with Marcus Aurelius as heir 139–61)
Marcus Aurelius	161–80 (with Lucius Verus as co-emperor 161–9; and Commodus as co-emperor 177–80)
Commodus	(with Aurelius from 177) 180–92
Septimius Severus	193–211 (with Caracalla as co-emperor 198–211, and with Geta as well 210–11)
Caracalla	(with Severus from 198) 211–17
Elagabalus	218–22
Severus Alexander	222–35
Maximinus I	235–8
Gordian III	238–44
Philip I	244–49
Diocletian	284–305 (with Maximianus as co-emperor in the west 286–305, assisted by Constantius Chlorus 293–305)
Carausius	286–93 (usurps in Britain only)
Allectus	293–6 (murderer and successor of Carausius)
Constantine I	307–37
Valentinian I	364–75 (with Valens in the East)
Theodosius I	379–95
Magnus Maximus	383–88 (usurper in Britain and the West)
Honorius	393–408 (with Arcadius in the East)
Constantine III	407–11 (usurper in Britain and the West)

25. Governors of Roman Britain from Trajan to Gordian III

This list has been drawn up from a variety of sources, and I am particularly grateful to Dr Margaret Roxan for supplying up-to-date information from military diplomas. Date-ranges are approximate only; *RIB* often supplies dates which are more exact but usually on the basis of inference or restoration, e.g. *RIB* 2192 which has no dating information on it at all. Inscriptions where the governor's name has been inferred and does not survive in any visible form have been omitted. The vast majority of these inscriptions are from the Wall, its forts or its hinterland and outpost forts. Only diplomas supply precise dates during tenure of office and are, at the time of writing, the most fertile source of new information.

Titus Avidius Quietus	98?–102? Diploma of 98 (*CIL* XVI, 43)
Lucius Neratius Marcellus	102?–6? Diploma 19 January 103 (*CIL* XVI, 98)
Marcus Atilius Metilius Bradua	Trajan/Hadrian. Perhaps 114–18. See Birley 1979, 170

Quintus Pompeius Falco	118?–22? Not testified on a British inscription but named as predecessor on the diploma of 17 July 122 (see next entry)
Aulus Platorius Nepos	122–6. *RIB* 1340, 1427, 1634, 1637, 1638, 1666, 1935 Diplomas 17 July 122 and 15? September 124 (*CIL* XVI, 69–70; *Lactor* 33. See Source 2)
Trebius Germanus	126–30. Diploma (20 August 127 – see Source 6), and possibly *RIB* 995 (unrestorable but either Nepos or Germanus)
Sextus Julius Severus?	130–4. *RIB* 739, 1550 (? see Source 6)
Publius Mummius Sisenna	134–8. Diploma 14 April 135 (*CIL* XVI, 82; and Birley 1979, 173. See Source 6)
Quintus Lollius Urbicus	138–42? *SHA* (see Source 9) *RIB* 1147, 1148(?), 1276, 2191, 2192
Cnaeus Papirius Aelianus	142?–6. Diploma dated between 10 December 145 and 9 December 146 (*CIL* XVI, 93)
Cnaeus Julius Verus	158. Diploma 27 February 158 (Holder, forthcoming) *RIB* 283, 1132, 1322 (see Source 11), 2110 (see Source 11)
... anus	154 or 159. Diploma (*CIL* XVI, 130)
Marcus Statius Priscus	161–2. Only known from a career inscription (Birley 1979, 174)
Sextus Calpurnius Agricola	163. *SHA* (c.163 – see Source 12) *RIB* 1137, 1149 (see Source 12), 1703, 1792 (see Source 13)
Quintus Antistius Adventus	–176. *RIB* 1083 (not later than November 176 but emperor not specified)
Ulpius Marcellus	176?–84. Diploma 23 March 178 (unpublished) Dio (180 – see Source 15) *RIB* 1329, 1463–4
Publius Helvius Pertinax	c.185. *SHA. Pertinax* iii.5
Clodius Albinus	c.192–7. Dio 73.xiv.3
Virius Lupus	c.197–202. Dio 75.v.4. *RIB* 637, 730, 1163
Caius Valerius Pudens	205. (Frere 1987, 157 – *JRS* 1961)
Lucius Alfenus Senecio	205–7. *RIB* 722, 723, 740, 746, 1151(?), 1234, 1337, 1462, 1909 (see Source 18)
Caius Julius Marcus	213. *RIB* 905, 976(?), 977(?), 1202 (erased), 1235 (erased), 1265 (erased), 2298
*[Marcus Antonius Gor?]dianus	216. *RIB* 590 (? erased), 1049, 1279 (? erased)
*Modius Julius	Early 3rd century. *RIB* 1914 (see Source 20)
*Tiberius Claudius Paulinus	220. *RIB* 1280
*Marius Valerianus	222. *RIB* 978, 1060, 1465
*Claudius Xenophon	222–3. *RIB* 1467, 1706, 2299, 2306
*... Maximus	225. *RIB* 1738
*Calvisius Rufus	225–35. *RIB* 929
*Valerius Crescens Fulvianus	225–35. *RIB* 587
*Claudius Apellinus	225–35. *RIB* 1281
*[T?]uccianus	237. *RIB* 1553
*Maecilius Fuscus	238–44. *RIB* 1092
*Egnatius Lucilianus	238–44. *RIB* 1091, 1262
*Nonius Philippus	242. *RIB* 897

* By c.215+ Britain was divided into two provinces: *Britannia Inferior* (the north) and *Britannia Superior* (the south), though this probably actually occurred under Septimius Severus before 211. The governors listed here were in charge of *Inferior*.

Select Bibliography

So many books and articles have been published on Hadrian's Wall that it would be impossible to include them all here. Instead, this Bibliography lists only the most important works, with additional material which has appeared in recent years. For a comprehensive summary of earlier material see E. Birley (1961), C. Daniels (1978), and D. Breeze and B. Dobson (1987) below under *General*. James Crow's *Housesteads* (1995), listed under *Forts* below, also has a detailed bibliography. Major articles on various features of Wall studies appear in the journal of the Society for the Promotion of Roman studies, called *Britannia*, as well as the local periodicals *Archaeologia Aeliana* (east) and *Transactions of the Cumberland and Westmorland Archaeological Society* (west).

Abbreviations

AA^4 = *Archaeologia Aeliana (4th series)*
Lactor no.4 = Maxfield, V., and Dobson, B., 1995 (see Inscriptions and other sources)
RIB = Collingwood and Wright, 1995 (see Inscriptions and other sources)
SHA = *Scriptores Historiae Augustae*, available in the Loeb Classics Series, Harvard University Press, Vols I and II (also in Penguin translation, *The Lives of the Later Caesars*, trans. by A. Birley, Penguin, London, 1976).

General
Birley, E., 1961, *Research on Hadrian's Wall*, Kendal
Birley, A., 1979, *The People of Roman Britain*, London
Breeze, D.J., 1997, *Hadrian's Wall. A souvenir guide to the Roman Wall*, London (the English Heritage Guide, frequently revised)
Breeze, D.J., and Dobson, B., 1987, *Hadrian's Wall* (3rd edition), London
Bruce, J. Collingwood, 1853, *The Roman Wall*, London
Bruce, J. Collingwood, 1885, *The Hand-Book to the Roman Wall*, London and Newcastle (3rd edition)
Daniels, C., (Ed) 1978, *Handbook to the Roman Wall* (13th edition), Newcastle
Daniels, C., (Ed) 1989, *The Eleventh Pilgrimage of Hadrian's Wall*, Newcastle
Embleton, R., and Graham, F., 1984, *Hadrian's Wall in the Days of the Romans*, Newcastle
Forde-Johnston, J., 1977, *Hadrian's Wall*, London
Graham, F., 1984, *Hadrian's Wall in the Days of the Romans*, Newcastle
Green, D., 1992, *Discovering Hadrian's Wall*, Edinburgh
Hutton, W., 1813, *The History of the Roman Wall*, London (reprinted by F. Graham, Newcastle, 1990)
Johnson, S., 1989, *Hadrian's Wall*, London

Antonine Wall
Breeze, D.J., and Dobson, B., 1987, (3rd, revised, edition), *Hadrian's Wall*, London, 86–111
Hanson, W.S., and Maxwell, G.S., 1986, *Rome's North-West Frontier, the Antonine Wall*, Edinburgh
Keppie, L.J.F., 1982, 'The Antonine Wall 1960-1980', *Britannia* xiii, 91–111
Robertson, A.S., 1979, *The Antonine Wall*, Glasgow

Army
Breeze, D.J., and Dobson, B., 1985, 'Roman Military Deployment in North England', *Britannia* xvi, 1ff
Holder, P.A., 1982, *The Roman Army in Britain*, London
Webster, G., 1985, *The Roman Imperial Army* (3rd edition), London

Armaments
Campbell, D.B., 1984, '*Ballistaria* in first to mid-third century Britain: a reappraisal', *Britannia* xv, 75-84
see also Donaldson, G.H., 1990, under *Inscriptions* below

Baths
MacDonald, G., 1931, 'The Bath-house at the Fort of Chesters (Cilurnum)', *AA⁴* viii, 219–304 (also exists as an off-print)

Bridges and other water-related topics
Bidwell, P., and Holbrook, N., 1989, *Hadrian's Wall bridges*, English Heritage, London (an in-depth study of recent work on the bridges on Hadrian's Wall and associated topics)
Biggins, J.A., and Taylor, D.J.A., 1999, 'A survey of the Roman fort and settlement at Birdoswald, Cumbria', *Britannia xx*, 91-100
Mackay, D.A. 1990, 'The Great Chesters Aqueduct: A New Survey', *Britannia* xxi, 285ff
Simpson, F. Gerald, 1976, *Watermills and Military Works on Hadrian's Wall. Excavations in Northumberland 1907–1913*, (edited by Grace Simpson), Kendal

Environment
Dumayne, L., 1994, 'The Effect of the Roman Occupation on the Environment of Hadrian's Wall: A Pollen Diagram from Fozy Moss, Northumbria', *Britannia* xxv, 217ff
see also Wilmott, T., under *Forts* below

Forts
Allason-Jones, L., and Miket, R., 1984, *The Catalogue of Small Finds from South Shields Roman Fort*, Newcastle
Bidwell, P.T., 1985, *The Roman Fort of Vindolanda at Chesterholm, Northumberland*, London
Birley, R., 1977, *Vindolanda. A Roman frontier post on Hadrian's Wall*, London
Bishop, M.C., and Dore, J.N., 1988, *Roman Corbridge: the Fort and Town*, London
Breeze, D.J., and Dobson, B., 1969, 'Fort types on Hadrian's Wall', *AA⁴* xlvii, 15ff
Crow, J., 1995, *Housesteads*, London (contains an extensive bibliography of various articles and accounts of this fort)
Robertson, A.S., 1975, *Birrens. Blatobulgium*, Edinburgh
Simpson, F.G., and Richmond, I.A., 1941, 'The Roman Fort on Hadrian's Wall at Benwell', *AA⁴* xix, 37 ff
Wilmott, T., 1997, *Excavations of a Roman fort* [Birdoswald] *on Hadrian's Wall and its successor settlements: 1987–92*, London
see also A. Birley (1961), C. Daniels (1978), and D. Breeze and B. Dobson (1987) under *General* above

Inscriptions and other sources
Bowman, A.K. 1994, *Life and Letters on the Roman Frontier. Vindolanda and its People*, London
Bowman, A.K., and Thomas, J.D., 1983, *Vindolanda: the Latin Writing Tablets*, Britannia Monograph no. 4
Bowman, A.K., Thomas, J.D., 1996, 'New Writing-Tablets from Vindolanda', *Britannia* xxvii, 299ff
Collingwood, R.G., and Wright, R.P., 1995, *The Roman Inscriptions of Britain. Volume I Inscriptions on Stone* (second edition, with *Addenda and Corrigenda* by R.S.O. Tomlin), Stroud (this is the definitive publication of all inscribed slabs, altars and so on. Wall and associated sites are represented from pp. 349–649 inclusive)
see also in *Britannia* xi (1980), 405 for the Newcastle garrison of Cubernians in AD 213; *ibid.* xxiii (1992), 318, for the inscription recording VIII and XXII Legions at Birrens; and *ibid.* xxvi (1995), 379–80, for the VI Legion inscription at South Shields
Donaldson, G.H., 1990, 'A Reinterpretation of *RIB* 1912 from Birdoswald', *Britannia* xxi, 207ff

Ireland, S., 1986, *Roman Britain. A Sourcebook*, Croom Helm, London (a comprehensive gathering of literary, epigraphic, and numismatic evidence for Roman Britain including many items and passages connected with the Wall)

Maxfield, V., and Dobson, B., 1995, *Inscriptions of Roman Britain, Lactor no.4* (third edition), London (a selection of Romano-British written records which includes Vindolanda tablets, diplomas, and stone inscriptions – available from the Lactor Publications Secretary, 5 Normington Close, Leigham Court Road, London SW16 2QS)

see also Loeb Classical Library, *Scriptores Historiae Augustae*, volume I (Hadrian, Antoninus Pius, and Septimius Severus), trans. David Magie, Harvard

Logistics

Kendal, R., 1996, 'Transport Logistics Associated with the Building of Hadrian's Wall', *Britannia* xxvii, 129ff

Mann, J.C. 1990, 'Hadrian's Wall West of the Irthing: The Role of VI Victrix', *Britannia* xxi, 289ff

Milecastles

Harbottle, B., Fraser, R., and Burton, F.C. 1988, 'The Westgate Road milecastle, Newcastle-upon-Tyne', *Britannia* xix, 153ff

see also A. Birley (1961), C. Daniels (1978), and D. Breeze and B. Dobson (1987) under *General* above

Temples and shrines

Allason-Jones, L., and McKay, B., 1985, *Coventina's Well*, Chesters

Richmond, I.A., and Gillam, J.P., 1951, 'The Temple of Mithras at Carrawburgh', AA^4 xxix, 1-92

Simpson, F.G., and Richmond, I.A., 1941, 'The Roman Fort on Hadrian's Wall at Benwell', AA^4 xix, 37 ff

Smith, D.J., 1962, 'The Shrine of the Nymphs and the Genius Loci at Carrawburgh', AA^4 xl, 59-81.

Turrets

Allason-Jones, L., 1988, '"Small Finds" from Turrets on Hadrian's Wall' in *Military Equipment and the Identity of Roman Soldiers*. Proceedings of the Fourth Roman Military Equipment Conference, ed. J.C. Coulston. *British Archaeological Reports (International Series)* no. 394, 1988, 197ff.

Crow, J.G., 1991, 'A Review of Current Research on the Turrets and Curtain of Hadrian's Wall', *Britannia* xxii, 51ff

see also A. Birley (1961), C. Daniels (1978), and D. Breeze and B. Dobson (1987) under *General* above

see also Current Archaeology

no. 96, 1985, 16–19: foundations and whitewashing

no. 108, 1988, 14–17: Peel Gap tower

no. 116, 1989: special edition concerned entirely with recent work on or near the Wall at Carlisle, Birdoswald, Vindolanda, Wallsend and South Shields

no. 128, 1992: Vindolanda

no. 132, 1993: Vindolanda

no. 133, 1993: South Shields

no. 153, 1997: Vindolanda

Glossary

Agger	The raised mound of a Roman road
Ala	A 'wing', used to describe a Roman auxiliary cavalry unit
Ansate	A panel, usually an inscription, with triangular projections on either side
Ashlar	Dressed stonework
Auxilia	Roman troops, normally non-citizens
Ballista	Catapult resembling a very large crossbow (also spelled *ballistra*)
Ballistarium	Derived from *ballista*, a catapult, and may mean either a workshop associated with production of artillery equipment or perhaps a catapult emplacement
Caldarium	Hot room in a bath-suite
Cheiroballista	Small catapult similar to large crossbow (also spelled *cheiroballistra*)
Cohort	Roman auxiliary infantry unit (*cohors*)
Cuneus	Roman auxiliary irregular cavalry unit
Damnatio memoriae	'Damnation of his memory', normally expressed by erasing an individual's name from inscriptions
Denarius	Silver coin around the size of a modern penny. At the end of the first century a Roman legionary was paid 225 a year but this figure was steadily raised. Auxiliaries were paid significantly less
Diploma	Inscribed bronze tablet, about 130mm by 130mm, recording the official honourable discharge of troops after 25 years service, and the grant of privileges. These privileges included citizenship for each man, his children, and the legalisation of his marriage. Diplomas (*diplomata*) name the units, the men concerned, the emperor, the governor, and are normally dated to a specific day and year; they are consequently exceptionally useful sources of evidence for provincial governors and garrisons. The tablet was fastened to another, bearing the names of witnesses, and sealed to ensure its authenticity. Each diploma was a miniature copy of the original set up in Rome. The term is a modern one, using the Latin word for an official letter of recommendation or favour written by the emperor or a magistrate
Frigidarium	Cold room in a bath-suite, normally a cold plunge pool
Horreum	Granary
Hypocaust	Heating system based on the transmission of hot air through channels under floors and within walls
Laconicum	Dry-heat room in a bath-suite
Milecastle	Walled enclosure appearing every Roman mile attached to the south face of the Wall with a gate in the north (Wall) and south sides, enclosing about 250–300 square metres. The term is entirely modern and has no Roman equivalent
Notitia Dignitatum	Late Roman document, surviving in medieval copies, which lists Roman military units and their forts. It is compromised by gaps and mistakes but is nevertheless a vital source
Numerus	Irregular auxiliary infantry unit
Onager	Wheel-mounted siege engine with ammunition ejected from an arm powered by twisted ropes
Praetorium	Commanding officer's house
Principia	Fort headquarters building
Short axis	Applied to a milecastle where the dimension between the north and south gates is less than the width of the milecastle
Stanegate	Roman road running west from Corbridge
Tepidarium	Warm room in a bath-suite

Trajan's Column	Stone column in Rome with a stone relief spiralling all the way up, depicting various scenes from Trajan's campaigns. It is an exceptionally valuable source for Roman military activity and buildings. Casts of the relief are in the Victoria and Albert Museum in London
Triclinium	Dining room
Turret	Small tower built at $\frac{1}{2}$-mile intervals between milecastles on Hadrian's Wall. The term is entirely modern and has no Roman equivalent
Valetudinarium	Military hospital
Vallum	Literally a wall or rampart, but now used to describe the ditch and mound system to the south of Hadrian's Wall
Via Principalis	The main road across a Roman fort, passing in front of the ***principia***
Vicus	Civilian settlement outside a fort
Wing walls	Short stretches of Hadrian's Wall built on either side of a feature such as a **turret** to receive the Wall when it was completed

Index